JOURNAL OF COGNITION AND DEVELOPMENT

Volume 3, Number 1, 2002

A Special Issue in Honor of Katherine Nelson*

CONTENTS

*Note: The articles in this special issue were edited by P. Bauer, except for the
article by Bauer et al., which was edited by P. Zelazo.*

JOURNAL OF
COGNITION AND DEVELOPMENT

First published by Lawrence Erlbaum Associates, Inc.

This edition published 2013 by Psychology Press

Psychology Press
Taylor & Francis Group
711 Third Avenue
New York, NY 10017

Psychology Press
Taylor & Francis Group
27 Church Road, Hove
East Sussex BN3 2FA

Psychology Press is an imprint of the Taylor & Francis Group, an informa business

JOURNAL OF COGNITION AND DEVELOPMENT, 3(1), 1–3

INTRODUCTION

Katherine Nelson's Theoretical Vision

Robyn Fivush
Department of Psychology
Emory University

Judith A. Hudson
Department of Psychology
Rutgers, The State University of New Jersey

Joan M. Lucariello
Lynch School of Education
Boston College

This special issue of the *Journal of Cognition and Development* is a unique tribute to Katherine Nelson on the occasion of her retirement from the Graduate School of the City University of New York. Although the journal does not, as a rule, publish special issues of this kind, an exception is being made in this instance because of Katherine Nelson's special role in the history and development of this journal. Nelson was on the original editorial board when the journal was founded as *Cognitive Development* in 1985, was its second editor from the years 1990 to 1995, and has continued her role on the editorial board as the journal transitioned to the *Journal of Cognition and Development* last year. Under her editorship, the journal became one of the premiere journals publishing innovative theoretical and empirical work in cognitive development.

This issue honors more than Nelson's stewardship of the journal; without a doubt, Katherine Nelson has been one of the most influential developmental psychologists of our generation. In the three decades since she received her degree at the University of California, Los Angeles, her work has fundamentally changed

Requests for reprints should be sent to Robyn Fivush, Department of Psychology, Emory University, Atlanta, GA 30322. E-mail: psyrf@emory.edu

the way in which we understand cognitive development. Her contributions to the field have been recognized in a myriad of ways—most recently, she received the Award for Distinguished Scientific Contribution to Research in Child Development from the Society for Research in Child Development in April 1999. Rather than listing her many awards and accomplishments, however, in this brief introduction we frame the way in which Katherine Nelson's theoretical vision has led to a changing conception of development.

Beginning with Nelson's (1973) monograph, *Structure and Strategy in Learning to Talk,* she focused on a functional approach to development, as well as highlighting individual differences and pathways in the developmental process. Nelson drew our attention to the social, emotional, and cultural contexts in which children are learning specific skills to accomplish meaningful goals in ongoing interactions with others. Challenging the then-current Piagetian metaphor of a single mind learning about an objective world through actions on objects, Nelson focused our attention on how the social and cultural context in which a child is embedded facilitates the development of skills and strategies for creating meaning in the world. Thus, Nelson's early work on language learning focused on individual differences in the ways in which children enter the language system as a function of their social context and communicative goals. Moreover, this work underlined the idea that language, as a cognitive phenomenon, must be understood as emerging from children's developing understanding of the world around them.

These ideas were further elucidated in Nelson's work on concepts. In her highly influential *Psychological Review* paper (Nelson, 1974), she described the ways in which children's dawning cognitive systems emerge from the kinds of interactions in which they engage in every day. To understand how children acquire the concept of *ball,* for example, we need to understand how this concept *ball* is embedded in the events and interactions in which children participate. Concepts emerge from their functional core—the ways in which they are used to accomplish meaningful goals in the child's world. The study of children's ways of making sense of their everyday world was the foundation for Nelson's programmatic research on the development of generalized event representations, culminating in the volume, *Event Knowledge: Structure and Function in Development* (Nelson, 1986). The idea of generalized event representations, or scripts, is at once simple and powerful, describing the content and organization of children's understanding about everyday events and interactions based on their narratives of familiar and routine events. The idea of simply asking preschool children to talk about events they have experienced in their lives was a radical idea in the early 1980s. Yet the knowledge derived from this work is formidable, fundamentally changing the conception of early cognitive development.

Throughout her career, Nelson maintained her basic theoretical insight into the role of meaning making in cognitive development, with children striving after meaning in their everyday interactions. Nelson's (1996) book, *Language in Cogni-*

tive Development: The Emergence of the Mediated Mind, is an expansive and impressive theoretical account of the role of language and social interaction in individual development. The themes that emerged early in Nelson's work are elaborated and expanded. Making sense of events occurs within social interactions in which adults mediate children's cognitive processes. Just as her first major theoretical contribution on individual pathways into language underscored, Nelson's more developed theoretical vision lays out the ways in which the kinds of social interactions in which children engage exert a powerful mediating influence on the kinds of skills they will develop and the kinds of meanings they will construct. Language is both a tool and a process by which we make sense of the world, and we do this through interacting with others.

Nelson has focused the field on process and pathways. Her core questions focus on how children make sense of the world around them and how sense making is embedded in ongoing everyday interactions with the objects and people in their world. In this special issue, three of Katherine's doctoral students (Fivush, Hudson, and Lucariello) and two additional scholars (Bauer and Tomasello) who have been highly influenced by her work contribute articles that highlight the ways in which Katherine's theoretical vision is currently being realized in ongoing research programs in developmental psychology.

Equally important, Nelson carries her core theoretical beliefs into the way she mentors. As her students and colleagues, we have been the recipients of sensitive scaffolding, with a mentor who gave us the freedom and the flexibility to find our own meaning. In this issue, we gratefully acknowledge all that Katherine Nelson has done for us individually, as well as what she has given the field. It is obvious that Nelson has changed the way we understand cognitive development. To us, it is also obvious how much she has changed us, both as people and as professionals. We are truly grateful.

REFERENCES

Nelson, K. (1973). Structure and strategy in learning to talk. *Society for Research in Child Development Monographs, 38*(12, Serial No. 149).

Nelson, K. (1974). Concept, word, and sentence: Interrelations in acquisition and development. *Psychological Review, 81,* 267–285.

Nelson, K. (1986). *Event knowledge: Structure and function in development.* Hillsdale, NJ: Lawrence Erlbaum Associates, Inc.

Nelson, K. (1996). *Language in cognitive development: The emergence of the mediated mind.* New York: Cambridge University Press.

JOURNAL OF COGNITION AND DEVELOPMENT, 3(1), 5–19

Things Are What They Do: Katherine Nelson's Functional Approach to Language and Cognition

Michael Tomasello
Department of Developmental and Comparative Psychology
Max Planck Institute for Evolutionary Anthropology
Leipzig, Germany

This article attempts to summarize Katherine Nelson's theoretical and empirical contributions to the ontogenetic study of language and cognition. Nelson's approach has consistently emphasized the function of language and linguistic concepts in children's larger conceptual and social lives and, conversely, how children's emerging understanding of the function of linguistic symbols in larger conceptual and social structures makes language acquisition possible in the first place. This approach has led to an especially fruitful body of theoretical and empirical work.

Suppose a Martian landed on Earth, came across a traffic light, and wanted to know what it was. The Martian could observe its blinking colored lights, open it up and inspect the electrical wiring and light bulbs inside, and she could even examine it with an EEG or MEG to measure the amount of electrical activity in its various subcomponents. However, to know what a traffic light is, the Martian will at some point need to know about traffic. That is, she will need to know about what the traffic light does, including such things as why people drive vehicles in the ways that they do and why this activity needs to be regulated in the ways that it is. Said still another way, the Martian will need to know what functions the traffic light serves in the larger cultural activities and events in which it is embedded.

Consistently throughout her scientific career, Katherine Nelson has argued that a human concept, especially a linguistically encoded concept, is similar to a traffic light—an artifact made by human beings for human purposes. It is, thus, similar to all artifacts, defined by its function in a more encompassing conceptual system

Requests for reprints should be sent to Michael Tomasello, Max Planck Institute for Evolutionary Anthropology, Inselstrasse 22, D–04103, Leipzig Germany. E-mail: tomas@eva.mpg.de

adapted to patterns of events and sociocultural activities in the human world. However, Nelson's consistency of focus has actually evolved through three periods in which she emphasized, in turn, the crucial role of (a) function (e.g., Nelson, 1974), (b) events (e.g., Nelson, 1985, 1986), and (c) culture (e.g., Nelson, 1996). The theoretical progression embodied in these three perspectives has resulted in an ever-more articulated account of many aspects of human cognitive development, but Nelson has paid special attention at all times to the complex and changing relations of language and cognition. In this article, I will try to explicate Nelson's approach to language and cognitive development by working through—briefly and in turn—each of these three perspectives.

FUNCTION

It has been known since Plato that the common sense view of concept formation has a logical problem. The common sense view holds that people form concepts simply by noticing similarities among things and thereby extracting some commonality, which constitutes the concept. The problem is that any given set of things has innumerably many similarities, and the concept-forming individual encounters these exemplars one at a time over time without any guidance about what to pay attention to. Therefore, when encountering the initial potential exemplars of a concept, the individual must already know what is the dimension of similarity to which he or she must attend or else he or she will become lost in the maze of possibilities at the outset. The point is that a totally bottom-up approach in which an individual person looks for similarities in a totally naive and unstructured way simply cannot work. It founders on the logical problem of circularity, because the concept to be formed must be implicitly presupposed if the individual is to focus his or her attention appropriately in its encounters with the initial potential exemplars.

The solution to this logical problem is to get some top-down processes working in concert with bottom-up processes. For example, Barsalou (1988) documented that people can form concepts based on goals, including ad hoc, temporary goals. Thus, a concept of "things to take on a picnic" would include such diverse items as fruit, a blanket, and a bottle opener, which all make sense because, and only because, people want to do certain kinds of things on picnics. More generally, Murphy and Medin (1985) argued that it is in terms of implicit theories that people form the vast majority of their concepts because such theories provide reasons for underlying similarities among exemplars. People's theories about the way things work tell them what to pay attention to and thus form the basis of the concept. Thus, a traffic light is a mechanical device that directs traffic in certain ways for certain purposes, and to decide if a particular thing in the world—for example, a device observed at intersections on Mars—is or is not a traffic light requires some judgements based on what this device does and how it does it.

Katherine Nelson saw all of this in the early 1970s. In her article in *Psychological Review* (Nelson, 1974) she proposed that children's first linguistic concepts derived in a straightforward manner from their already formed prelinguistic concepts. These prelinguistic concepts derived from children's understanding of what one can do with an object and what that object can do. This formed the functional core of the concept, whereas perceptual features were used to identify instances of the concept subsequently. In Nelson's extended example, she proposed that for children "ball" indicates things you can roll or bounce (among other things), and one could reliably identify balls by their round shape. Even in this early formulation, children's concepts were not conceptualized just in terms of the child's own actions (à la Piaget) but in terms of the functional relations the object had to other things in the environment as well.

This hypothesis made two major predictions. The first was that children's early word meanings would be based on function rather than form. A plethora of studies by Nelson and many other researchers tested this hypothesis, although sometimes with an incomplete understanding of the theory (see Nelson 1985, 1996, for thorough reviews). Some studies looked for word meanings based on functions the child could not possibly understand, and others took as evidence against the theory the fact that children notice new instances of a concept on the basis of perceptual features—when, in fact, the theory only claimed that functional features were the core of the concept. More recently, solid evidence for this proposal has come from a series of studies in which Kemler Nelson and colleagues (e.g., Kemler Nelson, Russell, Duke, & Jones, 2000) taught 2-year-old children novel names for novel artifacts that have novel functions—with these functions being related causally to perceptible aspects of the objects' physical structure. These researchers then investigated how children extended these names to new objects and found that, given only minimal experience with the new objects, children generalize the names in accordance with the objects' functions. Kemler Nelson et al. (2000) concluded that "two-year-olds name by function when they can make sense of the relation between the appearances and functions of artifacts" (p. 1271).

This aspect of the theory has also been upheld by the theoretical work of Mandler (2000) who argued that something is defined most fundamentally by what it does (e.g., a traffic light or a dog), with perceptual features serving an identifying function only. Based on a variety of her own studies as well as those of others, Mandler concluded that such conceptual categories are very different from the simple perceptual categories often studied in infants and nonhuman animals:

> Infants as young as 3 months of age form perceptual prototypes of objects ... [by] pulling out the main factors or principle components being presented ... Crucially, forming these kinds of perceptual categories or prototypes occurs without attention or intention and does not require conceptualization. Conceptual categorization, on the other hand, is concerned with setting up kinds, that is, with formulating what sorts

of things dogs or tables are ... This is a fundamental human capacity that differs from the ability to tell one thing apart from another ... As [infants] begin to encounter animals, vehicles, furniture, utensils, and so forth, they must form some idea of the meaning of these things, in particular characterizing the roles they play in events. The core of concept construction insofar as objects are concerned is characterizing what they do or what is done to them. (pp. 7–8)

The second prediction of the functional core hypothesis was that the child's early linguistic concepts were initially so bound up with functional knowledge that he or she would have trouble decontextualizing them for use in new situations. This hypothesis has also suffered from some misunderstandings. For example, Barrett, Harris, and Chasin (1991) found that children soon after their first birthdays generalize many of their earlier linguistic concepts beyond the initial learning contexts. However, these generalizations only concern the assimilation of novel objects to existing object concepts on the basis of perceptual similarity, which is not relevant to the issue of whether children can use their early words inside different functionally defined events. The fact is that Nelson's hypothesis that early words are "event bound" has never really been tested appropriately (i.e., with some reasonably rich definition of event), and indeed there are a multitude of observations that many of children's early words are event bound (e.g., Barrett, 1983). In any case, this feature of the theory is not inviolable, as Nelson (1996) herself clearly stated; children can in some cases generalize their concepts to novel events on the basis of only a few, or even just one, instance—if their event knowledge is of the right type.

Nelson went on to apply the very rich notion of function in a number of other creative ways, mostly involving the communicative or discourse function of linguistic concepts. First, Nelson's (1973) well-known analysis of individual differences in early language relied crucially on the notion of communicative function. In this case, Nelson proposed that some children generalize and understand the communicative function of words to be mainly referential, so they use them most often to simply name things. Other children come to understand the main function of words as expressive, so they use them most often to direct the attention or behavior of others. Although subsequent research has shown that these two types are not mutually exclusive—some children have nearly equal numbers of words used in each of these functions—it is still the case that there are children at each end of the continuum, and research into the reasons for their distinctive uses of language has yielded interesting insights into the nature of individual differences of language acquisition in general (for reviews, see Bates, Bretherton, & Snyder, 1988; Nelson, 1981; Shore, 1995).

In another well-known application of the theory, Nelson (1976) looked at children's early acquisition of adjectives. She identified three discourse functions in the way that children used words that adults would call adjectives: (a) as predications in utterances such as "This is big," (b) as modifiers in utterances such as "The big boy hit me," and (c) as classificatory modifiers in utterances such as "The baby moose" (where *baby* is most often a noun serving an adjectival function). The most interesting findings of this study was that 1- to 2-year-old children used different sets of specific words for these different functions. When Nelson looked at the independently coded words used in each of these three communicative functions, she found that more than 80% of the predications used by the less linguistically advanced children involved temporary states of objects or animate beings (e.g., broken, hurt). Only the more advanced children predicated a more diverse set of adjectives such as size, color, or descriptive properties. In contrast, children's modificational uses of adjectives mostly concerned descriptive properties (e.g., big, little) or evaluative properties (e.g., pretty, bad) from the beginning. Finally, the classificatory adjectives, used to subdivide referent classes, consisted of animate types (e.g., baby giraffe), substance terms (e.g., chocolate cookie), or kind terms (e.g., Panda bear)—again, mostly nouns used in adjectival functions. Because for any given child there was little overlap in the specific words used in these three functions, Nelson proposed that young children do not have a single class of adjectives, but rather they have three classes. The words are in classes depending on what they do communicatively. Similarly, and more recently, Pine and Lieven (1997) reported that young children use the definite and indefinite articles *a* and *the* with completely different sets of nouns.

Along the same lines, Nelson, Hampson, and Shaw (1993) looked more deeply into the well-known finding that English speaking children's early vocabularies are dominated by nouns. Once again, they looked more carefully at the specific words used and found some surprises. Specifically, they found that only about half of them were the prototypes that most theorists had in mind; that is, basic-level object categories (BLOCs) such as *dog* and *chair*—things you can hold or bump into. Just as frequent were nominals that did not refer to such tangible things (XBLOCs) such as *breakfast, kitchen, plastic, kiss, toy, lunch, light, park, doctor, night,* and *party.* This observation is significant because many theorists (e.g., Gentner, 1982) have claimed that the noun bias results from the fact that nouns indicate concrete objects, and concrete objects are more readily isolated and identified than actions and relations. This would not seem to hold for XBLOCs. Nelson's observations in this regard thus serve, once again, to focus our attention on the specifics on how different pieces of language function for young children—for example, to categorize objects, as in BLOCs, or to identify events, locations, and so forth, as in XBLOCs—even when they are from the same category in adult language.

As another part of this investigation (and treated in more detail by Nelson, 1995), Nelson identified a number of words in children's early vocabularies that could be used as either nouns or verbs. These so-called dual-category words included such common things as *bite, kiss, drink, walk, hug, help,* and *call.* Many children use some of these words for both functions, and most current theories of word learning and language development, or both, have basically no account of how they could do this, because they are based on the idea that children use form, and not function, as the starting point for category formation. Nelson's account was, quite simply, that young children often understand in context the different function being played by a given word (e.g., to refer or to predicate), and so in an important sense, the activity of drinking is a different concept from the thing being drunk, despite the fact that they are often associated with the same phonological sequence. In this case, it is hard to know how children could do this at all—how they could learn the two different meanings of *drink*—if function were not at the foundation of their linguistic representations.

Finally, Levy and Nelson (1994) investigated children's early acquisition of causal and temporal words, which most theories of lexical acquisition simply ignore. Examining children's earliest uses of such terms as *because, tomorrow, today, morning, pretty soon, yesterday,* and *now,* they found that children only use these terms in relatively formulaic phrases and for the same functions that their parents use them for. Thus, they hypothesized that in this case children's production of linguistic items preceded their comprehension, in the sense that their earliest uses were bound to specific discourse contexts and did not display adult-like flexibility of use. These words served discourse functions only, and a fully adult-like understanding awaits children's encounters with these words in a fuller range of functional contexts.

Even this brief account of this small subset of Nelson's empirical studies demonstrates that some aspects of early language acquisition can only be explained with explicit reference to the notion of function—both in the sense that underlying concepts have a functional core and in the sense that linguistic categories are formed on the basis of communicative–discourse function. These are both ideas on the cutting edge of current thinking about the relation of language to cognitive development (e.g., see the recent work of Slobin, 1991; Bowerman, 1993, on "thinking for speaking"; and Tomasello, 1992a, 1999, on grammatical category formation as "functionally based distributional analysis").

EVENTS

In the 1970s, Nelson discovered the theoretical construct of script, as developed by her Yale colleagues Roger Schank and Robert Abelson (1977; and also similar work by Fillmore and others on cognitive frames). As conceptual systems, scripts and frames provide an especially powerful top-down organizational component to human cognition. For example, if someone says, "Yesterday, I flew to New York," we do not believe that they flapped their arms and propelled themselves through the air, but rather the word *flew* invokes our commercial airline script. On the basis of invoking this script, we infer implicitly and automatically that the speaker bought a ticket, traveled to an airport, interacted with flight attendants, ate some tasteless snacks (and perhaps a tasteless meal), and so forth. Scripts and frames thus focus on cognitive organization in terms of events—rather than the object concepts that have so long dominated discussion in cognitive science—and provide a very powerful instrument for making inferences about the world on the basis of limited information.

Nelson (1985) applied the script concept to children's early cognitive development and meshed it with her notion of function. She posited that children's early cognition is organized most fundamentally in terms of events. Events include Piagetian sensory–motor actions, but importantly they include the social and cultural activities in which children participate as well. Thus, children fundamentally conceive their experience in terms of not only kissing and kicking, but also having breakfast and taking a bath. Events thus come in many shapes and sizes and so children's event representations do as well, with the commonality that all event representations are organized as sequences of actions or changes of state. Object concepts are derivative, in this account, in the sense that they must be extracted from these early event representations. It is important to emphasize that we are talking here not about the perception of objects and events but about their conceptualization (see the previous Mandler quotation). This point has been misunderstood by a number of Nelson's critics (see Nelson, 1985, 1996).

Following the lead of de Saussure (1916/1959), Nelson distinguished in these event representations a syntagmatic and a paradigmatic dimension. The sequential aspect of an event is its *syntagmatics,* the way the different participants in an event relate to one another spatially, temporally, and causally—thus forming the basis for a judgement about an element's function. For example, spoons and cereal relate to one another in specific ways in a breakfast script; spoons are used to pick up and transport things to the mouth and cereal is something to be transported to the mouth and eaten. The *paradigmatics* of an event concern the way that entities may substitute for one another in the various participant roles defined by an event; that is, things other than spoons may be used to transport food to the mouth and things other than cereal may be eaten. It is easy to see that the functional dimension of concept formation that Nelson focused on in her earlier work emerged naturally from the interplay between the syntagmatic and paradigmatic aspects of learning about events and their participant roles. In her words, "Balls are things that can play a specific functional role in a certain type of event. Something that looks like a ball but cannot fit into a 'ball event' is not a proper member of the paradigmatic set of balls" (Nelson, 1985, p. 182).

This is actually quite a novel proposal. Classically, concepts are formed on the basis of similarity and possibly other types of associations. In Nelson's account, children learn within events certain kinds of syntagmatic relations—and this is one dimension of cognitive organization—and then, the paradigmatic dimension enables them to also form relations of substitutability in events. Concepts formed on the basis of substitutability in events are called slot-filler categories, and they had been scarcely recognized before Nelson. This account is especially useful in explaining how young children form superordinate categories, such things as food and furniture in which members share little in common perceptually. Food consists simply of those items that play a certain role in children's breakfast, lunch, and dinner scripts.

In an especially well-known study, Lucariello, Kyratzis, and Nelson (1992) asked preschool children of various ages to provide specific items for five superordinate categories: food, clothes, animals, furniture, and tools. The first three of these in particular were hypothesized to have slot-filler structure because of their participation in salient events in children's lives, and indeed, it was found that the basis for each of these categories for young children was the similar events in which its exemplars participated. There was also evidence that the older children formed these categories on the basis of more different types of events than younger children. Subsequent research has shown that children can form both syntagmatic and paradigmatic categories from their initial event representations (see Nelson, 1996, for a review).

Nelson is one of the only theorists of children's language development who has gone onto focus on the nature of children's lexical development later in the preschool period (the one major exception being Anglin, 1977, 1983). Briefly, the idea is that by establishing lexical fields of similar terms, children construct relations such as synonymy, antonymy, and hyponymy (hierarchical relations). The establishment of these relations makes possible "the manipulation of language terms without reference to situational context" (Nelson, 1985, p. 214); that is, children establish lexical relations among words, "unencumbered by all of the syntagmatic entailments of the conceptual system" (Nelson, 1985, p. 214). Establishing these kinds of abstract relations enables children to, among other things, perform in adult-like ways in explicit verbal classification tasks as they approach school age. It is only at this point that Nelson is willing to say that children have "a system of semantic relations that is purely symbolic and semiautonomous, that is, it can operate independently of the conceptual system" (Nelson, 1985, p. 214). Strong evidence for this proposal was recently supplied by Sell (1992). In a study of children ranging in age from 2 to 10 years, she found that the youngest children seemed to possess mainly categories based in specific events. The slightly older children (5–6 years of age) possessed, in addition, slot-filler categories based on participant roles in whole classes of events. It was only the oldest, school-aged children, who possessed fully taxonomic conceptual categories independent of specific events and event types.

With respect to the grammatical structure of language, Tomasello (1992a) used Nelson's event-based model to explicate some aspects of children's early multiword productions. The hypothesis was that the basic structure of children's earliest multiword utterances is provided by verbs. The defining feature of verbs is of course the dynamic and sequential nature of their underlying conceptualizations; they refer to events and states of affairs. Moreover, the meaning of a verb perforce includes participant roles such as agent and patient as an integral component. For example, the meaning of the verb *give* includes the giver, the thing given, and the person given to as they engage in certain activities. Children's understanding and use of verbs, as event concepts, thus provides the structural backbone for their complex syntagmatic constructions, and paradigmatic categories of participants gain their significance in terms of the roles they play in these events.

Subsequent work on children's grammatical development has established two additional facts consistent with Nelson's general account. First, these early event–verb concepts are, to a large degree, context specific rather than general—so-called verb island organization (Tomasello, 1992a, 2000). Thus, English-speaking children learn many verb-island-type structures with open nominal slots; for example, X loves Y, X hates Y, X laughs, X cries, Y got broken, Y opened, and Y gave X to Z. Children's syntagmatic categories are thus such things as hitter, kisser, thing hit, thing kissed, and then later perhaps more general roles such as agent and patient. Second, children form paradigmatic linguistic categories of nouns earlier than verbs (Tomasello, Akhtar, Dodson, & Rekau, 1997), presumably because nominal terms substitute paradigmatically for one another more freely in children's utterances than do verbs. Thus, the formation of linguistic categories—both syntagmatic categories such as agent and patient and paradigmatic categories such as noun and verb—can be seen in the same basic terms as the formation of nonlinguistic (or semantic) categories. This is an important, and hitherto not often recognized, application of Nelson's theory to the study of children's language development.

For unknown reasons, cognitive scientists of all types have focused the vast majority of their attention on Linnéa hierarchies of object categories. Nelson—along with a few others such as Mandler (2000) and Gentner, Rattermann, Markman, and Kotovsky (1995)—however, has drawn our attention to the dynamic dimensions of human cognitive organization. This emphasis has opened up a number of new avenues of research that depend explicitly on the notion of event representations—perhaps most significantly the work on children's early memory and personal narratives as illustrated by many of the other articles in this issue (e.g., Fivush & Vasudeva, 2002/this issue; Hudson, 2002/this issue; Bauer, Wenner, & Kroupina, 2002/this issue), as well as by Nelson's own influential work on "narratives from the crib" (Nelson, 1989). Whether event representations should be seen as foundational for all aspects of human cognitive and linguistic development in the way Nelson proposed is a question for future research and theoretical discussion.

CULTURE

Implicit in all of Nelson's work, from the earliest publications, has been the insight that most of the activities that structure the immature person's life are recurrent cultural scripts and patterns. In her more recent work, this was fully explicit. With regard to word learning, for example, Nelson (1992) recently emphasized the role played by what she calls "contexted relevance." The idea is that children's understanding of novel pieces of language depends crucially on their understanding of how that piece of language fits in with is relevant to the ongoing social–communicative interaction in its particular social–cultural context (see also Tomasello, 1992b, 2001).

However, it was with her discovery of Donald (1991), resulting in her 1996 book, that Nelson's focus on culture became fully explicit. In Donald's theory, the primate mind in general is characterized by the perception of events, in episodic form tied to particular situations. At some point in evolution, human beings also began to represent the world mimetically, that is, to depict things and situations for others or the self through concrete actions as in gesture, dance, games, theater, and social ritual, and simple linguistic symbols. This later gave way to the mythic mind in that humans represent the world via narrative, and indeed the narrative motive to share experience of significant events with others is seen as the driving force behind the emergence of language in its modern form. Finally, theoretic representation involves the representation of information in external media such as books, pictures, maps, and explicit cultural models (e.g., scientific theories). The modern mind is a hybrid mind because it employs all four of these representational modalities.

Nelson (1996) attempted to construct an account of human cognitive ontogeny that paralleled Donald's (1991) phylogenetic–historical account, without, of course, falling into any naive form of recapitulationism. The general outline is as follows:

Infancy (0–1.5 years) = episodic
Early childhood (1.5–4 years) = mimetic
Middle childhood (4–10 years) = narrative
Adolescence (10 years–adult) = theoretic

With specific reference to language, the thesis is that before 4 years of age, children's language is based on episodic and mimetic representations, and so it is not truly symbolic and representational. That is, young children use language to direct and cajole, comment and question, request and exclaim, but they do not use it to represent the world explicitly as they will later when they, for example, report on a trip to the beach. Of course in one sense the language of 2-year-olds is symbolic and representational—"ball" is certainly a symbol for the real object—but it is symbolic in the sense of Karmiloff-Smith's (1992) procedural level of representation, and not in the sense of a more explicit, declarative level. Early language (e.g., that of 2-year-olds) occurs in the context of mimetic, and not narrative, activities, and so it is not fully representational:

Language … is used in, as part of, and in conjunction with [cultural] activities, and not primarily as a medium of conveying knowledge from one person to another. Its primary use is pragmatic, not symbolic ... Language uses in these shared activities help to mark them, to move them forward, but language is not initially used to *represent* them as such in the child's cognitive or communicative productions. (Nelson, 1996, p. 91)

The representational use of language is thus explicitly identified with narrative. Before they can engage in narrative discourse, children use language in the context of sensory–motor and mimetic activities, in effect letting those activities do much of the talking. On the other hand, when older children report on some event in which they have previously participated, the only representational medium is language, and it does virtually all of the representational work. Said another way, 2-year-olds are mostly communicating within the event in which they are currently participating—from inside the event, as it were. Five-year-olds sometimes communicate about events that are not ongoing—from an outside perspective—even expressing their own current attitude to that event. Older children thus use language not just to participate in and influence events, but also to depict them and comment on them for others linguistically.

The limited functions of early child language also result in children's inability to entertain multiple representations of an event simultaneously. That is, 3-year-olds can update or even build a mental representation (MREP) of an event on the basis of someone else's linguistic description, but they cannot consider simultaneously their own MREP of an event and the different representation of that event by another person as it is expressed linguistically. Older children are able to compare and contrast their own and another person's representations of an event because they now have made a clear distinction between MREPs and linguistic representations.

At this point, then, children will have developed basic skills in using linguistic LREPs [linguistic representations] to build novel MREPs that are different from those they have constructed from their own direct experience, and they will be able to move back and forth between their own basic event MREPs, the linguistic LREPs of those representations, and the linguistic LREPs of other people, whose representation of an event may differ from their own. (Nelson, 1996, p. 130)

The basic picture is that before 4 years of age, children use language "inside" socially shared events, but after that age they can also use language to depict and comment on these events for others—or, conversely, to comprehend the events linguistically expressed by others and relate them to their own MREPs.

The process driving this developmental progression is dialogue with more-or-less mature members of the culture, who possess hybrid minds incorporating all types of MREPs and cultural knowledge of events, and who thus react to the child's linguistic productions in ways that assume an adult conception of the world and culture. In true Vygotskian fashion, the external and interpersonal dialogue is internalized, and at the same time it is differentiated from and coordinated with the child's MREPs based on his or her own direct experience. What opens up for the child at this point is the whole world of culture that is expressed exclusively in linguistic form: from stories and myths to history and science. Interestingly, this process may influence children's social cognition directly as well. For example, children may notice discrepancies between their own use of words and that of others, they may come to comprehend mental state terms in the language, and they may experience direct instruction from adults on how to understand others. The reason that children fail false-belief tasks before 4 years of age—to address a currently hot topic—is simply that they cannot entertain simultaneously their own MREP of an event and another person's linguistic representation of that same event (Nelson, 1996).

One of the most distinctive characteristics of Nelson's approach to language acquisition and its relation to cognitive development is thus the contention that much of importance happens at older ages. In the lexicon, children are working well into school age at establishing semantic fields and the various kinds of interrelations among the lexical concepts in them. Moreover, children's emerging narrative skills, which also reach the critical point near school age, lead to new relations between linguistic and conceptual representations and to new ways for the child to conceptualize the mental states and prepositional attitudes of other persons. Virtually no other theorist has such a consistent and coherent account of linguistic and cognitive development that spans such an extended period of ontogenetic time.

Any theory attempting to cover such a broad sweep of developmental phenomena will perforce be lacking in detail in some areas, and Nelson's is no exception. Thus, most theorists think it a bit misleading to say that before 4 years of age children's language is pragmatic and not symbolic and representational. To be consistent, Nelson might say that the language of 2- and 3-year-olds is representational in a mimetic sense; that is, it is used to represent different aspects of events as they are lived out. Following this ontogenetically, narrative is distinctive not because it is representational, but rather because it represents such complex and "distanced" content. Narrative allows discourse interactants to focus on some participant as it moves through a string of events over extended periods of time, and the narrator can take an outside perspective on that string of events to express his or her current attitude. Narrative is a special form of linguistic representation, but it is not the only form.

Moreover, Nelson had no detailed account of how interaction with other people leads children to understand language as a representational medium. That is, children's differentiation of the linguistic representations of others from their own MREPs may be seen as part and parcel of their developing "theory of mind," and so it is likely that the same social constructional processes are involved in the two cases. In this regard Nelson might have focused on the kinds of discourse interactions in which much work must be done to achieve a meeting of minds. To list the most obvious kinds may include the following:

1. Different words are used for the same phenomenon in different discourse circumstances (e.g., *doggie, toy, Spot,* or *thing*).
2. Different grammatical constructions are used depending on the partner's knowledge and expectations (e.g., the same event is described with an active or passive utterance depending on the previously established topic of speaker and interlocutor).
3. When others do not understand their language, children must reflect on the communication process and what went wrong (e.g., when queried "What?" they must decide whether and how to reformulate their utterance depending on what caused the miscommunication).

It is these kinds of interactive phenomena in which children directly confront different perspectives on the world and are forced to examine how language works if they are to connect these perspectives (Tomasello, 1999).

CONCLUSIONS

In the world after Piaget, students of cognitive development have turned increasingly in one of two directions. The first is neo-nativism, in that those aspects of human cognition not dependent on specific experiences are investigated, catalogued, and related to subsequent developments. The second is cultural psychology, in which other aspects of human cognition—perhaps especially the Vygotskian "higher" psychological functions—are investigated as they emerge from children's interactions with adults and cultural artifacts in the socially shared events that comprise their daily lives. The main problem with each of these approaches is that it ignores the other. Neo-nativism mostly does not take into account the fact that organisms inherit their environments as much as they inherit their genomes, and that such important cognitive functions as language require for their ontogeny a specific set of environmental experiences. Cultural psychology, at least in its most radical form, focuses only on social–cultural experiences, often with little concern for the kinds of individual cognitive skills that enable children to participate meaningfully in cultural activities in the first place.

The strength of Nelson's theoretical approach is that it attempts to do justice to both of these points of view. Although clearly not comfortable with any form of simplistic nativism, Nelson explicitly recognized that human infants develop a number of cognitive skills reflecting their primate heritage (e.g., event perception), and they do this essentially on the basis of their own experience. On the other hand, language and other cultural skills could only have evolved socially, and children can only learn these skills through social interaction. The result is a hybrid mind, à la Donald, that both retains its foundation in individual experience, but then learns new things through participation in culture and language. Nelson was able to bridge the sometimes considerable gap between straight cognitivists and culturalists because she focused on events as the foundational experiential units, and events that can be used to characterize both individual experience and the social activities in which children acquire the majority of their cultural skills (see also Tomasello, 1999).

Overall, Nelson's empirical and theoretical work is among the most important in the study of language and cognitive development. This is mainly because it provides an event-based, socially-based counterpoint to the excessive focus on individuals and objects that characterizes many neo-Piagetian and neo-nativist approaches, and indeed it incorporates these approaches to some extent, without slipping into any excessive forms of social constructivism. Nelson's work is thus among the most important on the current scene in helping us to understand how people proceed ontogenetically from the individually based cognition characteristic of primates in general to the kinds of collective cognition, embodied in language and other cultural artifacts, that characterizes mature Homo sapiens.

REFERENCES

Anglin, J. (1977). *Word, object, and conceptual development*. New York: Norton.

Anglin, J. (1983). Extensional aspects of the preschool child's word concepts. In T. Seiter & W. Wannemacher (Eds.), *Concept development and the development of word meaning* (pp. 125–152). New York: Springer Verlag.

Barrett, M. (1983). The early acquisition and development of the meanings of action-related words. In T. Seiler & W. Wannenmacher (Eds.), *Concept development and the acquisition of word meaning* (pp. 14–35). Berlin, Germany: Springer-Verlag.

Barrett, M., Harris, M., & Chasin, J. (1991). Early lexical development and maternal speech: A comparison of children's initial and subsequent use of words. *Journal of Child Language, 18*, 21–40.

Barsalou, L. (1988). Frames, concepts, and conceptual fields. In A. Lehrer & E. Kittay (Eds.), *Frames, fields, and contrast*. Hillsdale, NJ: Lawrence Erlbaum Associates, Inc.

Bates, E., Bretherton, I., & Snyder, L. (1988). *From first words to grammar: Individual differences and dissociable mechanisms*. Cambridge, England: Cambridge University Press.

Bowerman, M. (1993). Typological perspectives on language acquisition: Do crosslinguistic patterns predict development. In E. V. Clark (Ed.), *Proceedings of the 25th annual Child Language Research Forum* (pp. 1–21). New York: Cambridge University Press.

de Saussure, F. (1959). *Course in general linguistics*. New York: Philosophical Library. (Original work published 1916)

Donald, M. (1991). *Origins of the modern mind*. Cambridge, MA: Harvard University Press.

Gentner, D. (1982). Why nouns are learned before verbs: Linguistic relativity versus natural partitioning. In S. Kuczaj (Ed.), *Language development* (Vol. 2, pp. 210–254). Hillsdale, NJ: Lawrence Erlbaum Associates, Inc.

Gentner, D., Rattermann, M. J., Markman, A., & Kotovsky, L. (1995). Two forces in the development of relational similarity. In T. J. Simon & G. S. Halford (Eds.), *Developing cognitive competence: New approaches to process modeling* (pp. 263–313). Hillsdale, NJ: Lawrence Erlbaum Associates, Inc.

Karmiloff-Smith, A. (1992). *Beyond modularity: A developmental perspective on cognitive science.* Cambridge, MA: MIT Press.

Kemler Nelson, D., Russell, R., Duke, N., & Jones, K. (2000). Two-year-olds will name artifacts by their functions. *Child Development, 71,* 1271–1288.

Levy, E., & Nelson, K. (1994). Words in discourse: A dialectical approach to the acquisition of meaning and use. *Journal of Child Language, 21,* 367–389.

Lucariello, J., Kyratzis, A., & Nelson, K. (1992). Taxonomic knowledge: What kind and when. *Child Development, 63,* 978–998.

Mandler, J. (2000). Perceptual and conceptual processes in infancy. *Journal of Cognition and Development, 1,* 3–36.

Murphy, G., & Medin, D. (1985). The role of theories in conceptual coherence. *Psychological Review, 92,* 289–316.

Nelson, K. (1973). Structure and strategy in learning to talk. *Monographs of the Society for Research in Child Development, 38*(No. 149).

Nelson, K. (1974). Concept, word, and sentence: Interrelations in acquisition and development. *Psychological Review, 81,* 267–285.

Nelson, K. (1976). Some attributes of adjectives used by young children. *Cognition, 7,* 461–479.

Nelson, K. (1981). Individual differences in language development: Implications for development and language. *Developmental Psychology, 17,* 170–187.

Nelson, K. (1985). *Making sense: The acquisition of shared meaning.* New York: Academic.

Nelson, K. (Ed.). (1986). *Event knowledge: Structure and function in development.* Hillsdale, NJ: Lawrence Erlbaum Associates, Inc.

Nelson, K. (Ed.). (1989). *Narratives from the crib.* Cambridge, MA: Harvard University Press.

Nelson, K. (1992, August). *Contexted relevance and the acquisition of shared meaning.* Paper presented at the British Child Language Seminar, Glasgow, Scotland.

Nelson, K. (1995). The dual category problem in the acquisition of action words. In M. Tomasello & W. Merriman (Eds.), *Beyond names for things: Young children's acquisition of verbs* (pp. 311–339). Mahwah, NJ: Lawrence Erlbaum Associates, Inc.

Nelson, K. (1996). *Language in cognitive development.* New York: Cambridge University Press.

Nelson, K., Hampson, J., & Shaw, L. (1993). Nouns in early lexicons: Evidence, explanations and implications. *Journal of Child Language, 20,* 61–84.

Pine, J., & Lieven, E. (1997). Slot and frame patterns in the development of the determiner category. *Applied Psycholinguistics, 18,* 123–138.

Schank, R., & Abelson, R. (1977). *Scripts, plans, goals and understanding.* Hillsdale, NJ: Lawrence Erlbaum Associates, Inc.

Sell, M. (1992). The development of children's knowledge structures: Events, slots, and taxonomies. *Journal of Child Language, 19,* 659–676.

Shore, C. (1995). *Individual differences in language development.* London: Sage.

Slobin, D. (1991). Learning to think for speaking: Native language, cognition, and rhetorical style. *Pragmatics, 1,* 7–26.

Tomasello, M. (1992a). *First verbs: A case study of early grammatical development.* New York: Cambridge University Press.

Tomasello, M. (1992b). The social bases of language acquisition. *Social Development, 1,* 67–87.

Tomasello, M. (1999). *The cultural origins of human cognition.* Cambridge, MA: Harvard University Press.

Tomasello, M. (2000). Do young children have adult syntactic competence? *Cognition, 74,* 209–253.

Tomasello, M. (2001). Perceiving intentions and learning words in the second year of life. In M. Bowerman & S. Levinson (Eds.), *Language acquisition and conceptual development* (pp. 198–221). Cambridge, England: Cambridge University Press.

Tomasello, M., Akhtar, N., Dodson, K., & Rekau, L. (1997). Differential productivity in young children's use of nouns and verbs. *Journal of Child Language, 24,* 373–387.

JOURNAL OF COGNITION AND DEVELOPMENT, 3(1), 21–47

Making the Past Present: Later Verbal Accessibility of Early Memories

Patricia J. Bauer
Institute of Child Development
University of Minnesota

Jennifer A. Wenner
Department of Psychology
Macalester College

Maria G. Kroupina
Institute of Child Development
University of Minnesota

A major question in the literature regarding memory development is whether memories of events from early in life are later accessible to verbal report. In a controlled study, we examined this question in toddlers who were 13, 16, or 20 months old at the time of exposure to specific events, and who were evaluated for spontaneous verbal expression of memory after delays of 9 to 12 months (Experiment 1), or 1 to 3 months (Experiment 2). Verbal reports of the events were elicited at the age of 3 years (both experiments). There was little evidence of spontaneous verbal mnemonic expression at the first delayed-recall test; the mnemonic expression that was observed was predicted by concurrent age and concurrent verbal fluency. Children who had been 20 months at the time of first experience of the events, and who were older and more verbally fluent at the first delayed-recall test (i.e., 20-month-olds in Experiment 1), provided verbal evidence of event memory at 3 years. The results are consistent with the suggestion that under some circumstances, early memories later are accessible to verbal report.

For much of the history of cognitive and developmental science, it was widely assumed that young children were unable to form memories of events that would en-

Requests for reprints should be sent to Patricia J. Bauer, Institute of Child Development, 51 East River Road, University of Minnesota, Minneapolis, Minnesota 55455–0345. E-mail: pbauer@tc.umn.edu

dure and be accessible over time. In a highly influential series of studies, Nelson (1986) challenged this assumption and found it wanting. Spurred by reports of mnemonic competence in preschoolers and armed with nonverbal measures of memory, researchers expanded the search for early mnemonic competence to children younger than 3 years of age. Although the exploration has been fruitful indeed (see Bauer, in press-a, for a review), largely missing from the database on very young children's memories is evidence of an important component of older children's and adults' mnemonic function—namely, verbal accessibility. The ability to talk about a past event long has been viewed as a hallmark of declarative or explicit memory for the event. Moreover, as Nelson (1993) argued so compellingly, it is only memories that are verbally accessible that are available to become part of our personal memory system or autobiography. In this study, in recognition of the central role of language and verbal expression, we report the results of studies of long-term verbal accessibility of memories from the 2nd year of life.

Some of the earliest evidence of young children's mnemonic competence came from the Nelson and Ross (1980) diary studies and naturalistic observations (see also Ratner, 1980; Todd & Perlmutter, 1980). On its heels was Nelson and Gruendel's (1981, 1986) research that showed children as young as 3 years of age already had well-organized representations of familiar events, such as going to McDonald's®. These findings provided the impetus for examination of children's early memories of unique events, such as going to Disney World® (Hamond & Fivush, 1991; see also, e.g., Fivush, Gray, & Fromhoff, 1987). They also motivated work on basic mnemonic processes in children younger than 3 years of age: If 3-year-olds already evidence coherent memories of past events, the capacity to construct them must have developed earlier.

Because children younger than 3 years old cannot be counted on to provide verbal reports (although see Nelson's, 1989, report of Emily's crib talk), investigation of the earliest emergence of event memory required development of techniques that tapped explicit or declarative memory, but that were nonverbal. Elicited and deferred imitation are argued to provide a nonverbal means of assessing these processes (see Bauer, in press-b, for discussion). In imitation tasks, props are used to produce an action or sequence of actions the child is invited to imitate either immediately (*elicited imitation*), after a delay (*deferred imitation*), or both. Children's reproduction of the action or sequence of actions serves as the measure of recall.

Use of elicited and deferred imitation has revealed well-organized event memories in children as young as 9 months (e.g., Bauer, Wiebe, Waters, & Bangston, 2001; Carver & Bauer, 1999, in press). Over relatively short delays (e.g., 1 week), children evidence excellent memory for episodic features of events, such as the specific objects used in them (e.g., Bauer & Dow, 1994; Lechuga, Marcos-Ruiz, & Bauer, 2001), and the temporal order in which the sequences unfolded (e.g., Bauer, Hertsgaard, Dropik, & Daly, 1998). Children also retain event information over long delays. For example, children 13 months of age recall the actions of events for

6 months; children 16 and 20 months recall ordered sequences of action for as long as 9 and 12 months (e.g., Bauer, Wenner, Dropik, & Wewerka, 2000). These demonstrations make clear that by the second year children have available one of the foundational ingredients of autobiographical memory: a basic event knowledge system (Nelson, 1993).

Although great strides have been made in research on event memory in children younger than 3 years old, one source of evidence of memory that abounds in the literature on older children is conspicuously absent from that on younger children—verbal report. The absence of verbally accessible memories is relative, rather than absolute: Children can provide verbal reports of events from the distant past (e.g., Fivush et al., 1987). There are even occasional reports of children making reference to experiences that they had as preverbal infants. For example, Nelson and Ross (1980) reported instances in which 21- to 27-month-olds verbalized about events or objects they had experienced well before they were able to label them (see also Myers, Clifton, & Clarkson, 1987; Todd & Perlmutter, 1980).

One of a small number of studies that have focused on the question of whether early memories later are accessible to verbal report is Peterson and Rideout (1998). The researchers interviewed children about trips to the emergency room necessitated by accidents. The accidents occurred when the children were 13 to 35 months of age; the interviews were conducted shortly thereafter and again 6 months, 12 months, and 18 or 24 months later. Children who were 13 to 18 months of age at the time of their injuries were unable to provide verbal accounts, although at the later interviews, they had the requisite language ability. The authors attributed the children's difficulty in verbally describing their experiences to unavailability of a verbal means of encoding at the time of the event. In contrast, although the children who were injured between 20 and 25 months had not been able to describe their experiences at the time, they were able to provide verbal reports 6 months later. Some of the children maintained verbally accessible memories over the subsequent delays between interviews. Children who were 26 months or older at the time of the experience provided verbal reports at all delays.

Bauer, Kroupina, Schwade, Dropik, and Wewerka (1998; see also Bauer & Wewerka, 1995, 1997) served as a complement to Peterson and Rideout (1998). Bauer, Kroupina, et al. examined the later verbal accessibility of memories for events among a subset of children who participated in Bauer et al. (2000). Children were enrolled in the parent study at the ages of 13, 16, or 20 months, at which time they were exposed to novel multistep event sequences. The children were permitted to imitate half of the sequences one time; the other half of the sequences were tested in deferred fashion (i.e., imitation was permitted only after imposition of a delay). The children were tested for recall of the sequences after intervals of either 1, 3, 6, 9, or 12 months (see Bauer et al., 2000, for procedural details). At the time of enrollment and for most of the sample, at the delayed-recall test, parents of the children reported on their children's productive vocabularies, thereby providing task-independent assessments of children's language abilities.

As noted earlier (and as described in detail in Bauer et al., 2000), the 13-month-olds showed nonverbal evidence of memory for the actions of the sequences for 6 months; the 16- and 20-month-olds showed nonverbal temporally ordered recall for 9 months and 12 months. At the time of their nonverbal delayed-recall tests, although we did not elicit them, the children often produced verbalizations about the events. In Bauer, Kroupina, et al. (1998), for a subset of the 16- and 20-month-olds in the 6- and 12-month delay conditions, we characterized the children's spontaneous verbalizations as either indicative of memory or not indicative of memory. The children evidenced verbal memory for events that they had been permitted to imitate prior to imposition of the 6- or 12-month delays. The children who had been 20 months at the time of experience of the events also provided verbal evidence of memory for events that they had only watched. Across age groups, verbal expression of memory was related to concurrent verbal fluency. That is, spontaneous production of a relatively large number of utterances in the course of the test session was related to verbal mnemonic expression. In contrast to the results of Peterson and Rideout (1998), verbal mnemonic expression was not related to children's ages at enrollment, and nor was it related to the reported productive vocabulary at the time of enrollment.

The oldest children also were able to talk about the events after an additional delay averaging 11 months. As described in Bauer, Kroupina, et al. (1998), we tested the children a second time when they were 3 years old. The timing of the second delayed-recall test was selected based on the expectation that by age 3, the children could be relied on to participate in memory conversations (e.g., Fivush et al., 1987). Accordingly, at the second delayed-recall test we elicited verbal reports about the events. The children who had been, on average, 29 months at the first delayed-recall test (i.e., children enrolled at 20 months) provided verbal evidence of memory at age 3 years. In contrast, the children who had been, on average, 25 months at the first delayed-recall test (i.e., children enrolled at 16 months) did not. Although the younger children had experienced a longer period of time between the two delayed-recall tests, relative to the older children, the length of delay is an unlikely explanation for the absence of verbally accessible memories among the younger children: The length of time between tests was not correlated with verbal expression of memory. Rather, what predicted verbal mnemonic expression at age 3 was children's age at the time of the test and their previous verbal expression of memory (which, as noted earlier, was related to overall verbal fluency at the first test).

Bauer, Kroupina, et al. (1998) provided a virtually unprecedented controlled investigation of long-term verbal accessibility of early memories. The results imply that at least under some circumstances, memories originally likely encoded primarily nonlinguistically later can be described verbally. An important ingredient in later verbal accessibility appears to be the opportunity to apply currently available language to "embellish" or augment a memory representation. This possibility may rarely be realized, however, because the necessary circumstances are likely: Unless the event occurs again, or is reinstated in memory, the referent (the event itself) and the linguistic tokens that describe it are not simultaneously available and therefore, cannot be mapped onto one another. Although strictly verbal means are effective at reinstating memories in older children, they are not effective for young children (Hudson, 1993). Nevertheless, as observed by Nelson and Ross (1980), physical cues such as a familiar location or a person involved in an event, can reinstate memories even when language may not. Indeed, Bauer, Kroupina, et al. suggested that the opportunity for linguistic augmentation of early memories is afforded by the contextualized first delayed-recall test.

In this research, we furthered the investigation of later verbal accessibility in three ways. First, in Experiment 1, using an independent sample from the same parent study (i.e., Bauer et al., 2000), we conducted a test for replication of the patterns observed in Bauer, Kroupina, et al. (1998). Given both the significance of the question of later verbal accessibility of early memories, and the different patterns in Peterson and Rideout (1998) compared with Bauer, Kroupina, et al., a test for replication is essential. Second, in Experiment 2 we extended the investigation to children who had experienced especially long delays between the first and the second delayed-recall tests. Long delays provide a strong test of whether early memories later are verbally accessible. Third, in both experiments, we extended the investigation to children who had been only 13 months of age at the time of enrollment in the parent study. Extension of the inquiry to the youngest children in the sample is important because it provides a strong test of the role of language at the time of encoding on later verbal accessibility: As a group, the youngest children were the least verbal at the time of encoding of the events. Moreover, the youngest children experienced the longest delays between the first and the second delayed-recall tests.

GENERAL METHOD

The methods for recruitment and testing of participants and for coding of the data were the same for both experiments. Accordingly, we describe them here. Specific features that varied between experiments are described in the context of each experiment in turn.

Participants

The data were derived from a subset of children who participated in a larger study of long-term memory development (Bauer et al., 2000). The source of participants thus was the same as for Bauer, Kroupina, et al. (1998). There was no overlap in the samples in the two reports. As explained in the previous related reports, the majority of participants were White and from families of middle- and upper-middle class status.

Materials

Test events. The children were tested for recall of six multistep event sequences at delayed-recall Test 1, and nine multistep event sequences at delayed-recall Test 2. To accommodate developmental differences in the amount of information that children are able to remember (see Bauer et al., 2000, for discussion), children were exposed to sequences that were either three or four steps in length: All of the children enrolled at 20 months were exposed to four-step test events; children enrolled at 16 months were exposed to either four-step or three-step test events; all of the children enrolled at 13 months were exposed to three-step test events. In both experiments in this research, half of the children enrolled at 16 months were tested on three-step sequences and half on four-step sequences. The test events were of three types: (a) sequences completely temporally constrained (enabling); (b) sequences completely lacking in temporal constraints and thus, arbitrarily ordered (arbitrary); and (c) sequences that were a mixture of enabling and arbitrary temporal relations (mixed). Examples of each event type can be found in Bauer, Kroupina, et al. (1998); a complete listing and description of the test events is available in Bauer et al. (2000).

Vocabulary checklists. On enrollment, and again at delayed-recall Test 1, most of the children's parents completed the MacArthur Communicative Development Inventory. Parents were asked to indicate which words their children produced. The instruments have been validated and have considerable stability with respect to assessment of general linguistic sophistication (Fenson et al., 1994). Because there is no parental report measure for 3-year-olds that is comparable to that for children 30 months and younger, parental reports of productive vocabulary at delayed-recall Test 2 are not available.

Procedure

All of the children were seen in the laboratory for five 45- to 60-min sessions. The first three sessions (exposure sessions) each were separated by 1 week. The fourth session (delayed-recall Test 1) took place after preassigned delays that varied between experiments (see Table 1). The fifth session (delayed-recall Test 2) took place when the children were 36 to 52 months of age and a minimum of 4 months after delayed-recall Test 1 (see Table 1). One of two female experimenters conducted the first four sessions for each of the children (i.e., three exposure sessions

TABLE 1
Mean Ages and Ranges and Mean Delay Intervals and Ranges for Children in Experiments 1 and 2

| | Age | | | | | | Delay | | | |
| | Enrollment | | Delayed Test 1 | | Delayed Test 2 | | Original | | Test 1–2 | |
Experiment–Group	M	Range	M	Range	M	Range	M	Range	M	Range
Panel A: Experiment 1										
13 month	13;10	12;24–13;16	24;06	22;15–26;05	39;08	37;10–40;24	10;19	8;28–12;14	15;02	11;19–17;26
16 month	16;10	15;26–16;20	27;07	25;03–29;04	40;08	36;07–52;08	10;19	8;27–12;11	13;02	7;24–23;14
20 month	20;08	19;27–20;19	31;10	29;10–33;11	38;23	36;17–41;18	10;23	8;21–12;22	7;14	4;06–9;29
Panel B: Experiment 2										
13 month	13;12	13;06–13;18	14;16	12;05–16;25	38;04	36;06–41;05	1;29	0;30–3;01	23;18	19;17–27;15
16 month	16;09	15;13–16;14	18;14	17;05–20;11	37;21	36;05–40;20	2;09	0;29–3;06	19;06	17;12–21;18
20 month	20;13	20;10–20;17	22;25	21;18–24;05	38;29	36;22–41;11	2;03	0;28–3;07	16;04	13;23–19;23

Note. Ages are given in months;days.

and the delayed-recall Test 1); the children were tested by the same experimenter at each of the first four sessions. The children were tested by a different female experimenter at Session 5.[1]

Exposure sessions. For children in the target age range, memory over long delays is enhanced by repeated experience (e.g., Bauer, Hertsgaard, & Wewerka, 1995), so children were exposed to the six test sequences (two enabling, two mixed, and two arbitrary) at each of three sessions. Previous research also has revealed differences in recall as a function of whether children are allowed to imitate prior to imposition of a delay (Bauer et al., 1995). To assess the influence of mode of participation in an event on long-term recall and subsequent verbal accessibility, children watched, but did not imitate, three test events (one sequence of each type). Children were allowed to imitate the other three events (one sequence of each type) one time prior to the delay.

As described in detail in Bauer et al. (2000), at the first exposure session, for each event in turn, the experimenter first familiarized the children with the props by allowing them to manipulate them. After familiarization, she modeled the event, with narration, two times in succession. She then put the props away and presented the props for the next event. The session ended after presentation of all six events. At the second exposure session, the children again experienced two demonstrations of each event; they had no opportunity to interact with the props. For the first three events (watch condition), the third session was identical to the second. For the last three events, after modeling, the children were permitted to imitate the sequences.

Delayed-recall Test 1. For each of the six events in turn, the experimenter presented the props, and allowed the child to manipulate them. After a brief period, the experimenter prompted the child by providing the label given for the event at each exposure session: "You can make/do X with that stuff." At the end of the delayed-recall period, the experimenter modeled the sequence of actions, after which the children were invited to imitate. As a within-subjects control, following the

---

[1]Testing by a different experimenter at Sessions 1 to 4 versus Session 5 is a departure from the procedures employed in Bauer, Kroupina, et al. (1998), in which the children were tested by the same experimenter at all five sessions. The possible impact of the change in experimenter was evaluated using a separate sample of children originally enrolled at 16 months of age. We compared the verbal behavior of 10 children enrolled at 16 months and tested by the same experimenter at all five sessions with that of 10 children enrolled at 16 months and tested by the same experimenter at Sessions 1 to 4 and a different experimenter at Session 5. The number of utterances classified as mnemonic did not differ for the two groups. The children tested by a different experimenter at Session 5 produced a larger number of nonmnemonic utterances, relative to the children tested by the same experimenter at all sessions. Thus, being tested by a different experimenter at delayed-recall Test 2 had a neutral or even facilitating effect on children's levels of verbal production. Details of the analyses are available from Patricia J. Bauer.

same procedure, the children also were tested on three new events (one sequence of each type). Higher levels of performance on the old, compared with the new, events can be attributed to memory.

Delayed-recall Test 2.   As described by Bauer, Kroupina, et al. (1998), the procedure for the second delayed-recall test differed from the first in that before presenting the event-related props to the children (before props condition), the experimenter (one of whom was Jennifer A. Wenner) elicited verbal reports about the props and events. For each event in turn, the experimenter placed the props beyond the child's reach and asked, "What was this one called? What did we do with this?" Children were prompted to continue their reports with general statements such as "What else did we do?" Once the children either had completed a description of the event or appeared to have exhausted the effort, the props were given to them (after props condition). As a within-subjects control, following the same procedure, the children were tested on 3 new events (one sequence of each type), for a total of 12 events (3 originally imitated, 3 originally watched, 3 new at delayed-recall Test 1, and 3 new at delayed-recall Test 2).

Counterbalancing.   At delayed-recall Test 1, the nine test sequences (three imitated, three watched, and three new) were presented in order such that sessions never began or ended with a new event sequence. This was done to ensure that were they to obtain, lower levels of performance on the new sequences could not be due to warm up or fatigue effects. Within that constraint, the test sequences of the different types (enabling, mixed, and arbitrary) and in the different experience conditions (imitated, watched, and new) were interspersed with one another. In the parent study, each sequence was presented in each serial position approximately equally often (with the exception of new sequences, as noted). A similar procedure was followed at delayed-recall Test 2.

Scoring

All sessions were videotaped. From the videotapes we derived nonverbal and verbal measures of performance. Because the focus of this research is children's verbal memory for the events, neither the scoring of nonverbal performance nor the results associated with it are described (see Bauer et al., 2000, for details). Coders were not explicitly aware of the children's ages either at the time of exposure to the events or at the time of the delayed-recall tests. Moreover, they were unaware of (a) the delay interval, (b) whether a given event was old or new, and (c) the specific research hypotheses.

Estimations of children's productive vocabularies at the time of enrollment and at delayed-recall Test 1 were obtained by counting the total number of words on the MacArthur Communicative Development Inventory that parents indicated their children produced.

Children's verbalizations during the delayed-recall phases of each test session were transcribed (i.e., children's verbalizations during and after the experimenter remodeled the event sequences were not transcribed or coded). We then assigned each propositional unit to one of two categories (illustrated with reference to "Make a gong"):

1. Mnemonic utterances were propositional units judged to be indicative of memory for a test event. Instances included verbal behaviors in which the child (a) named or described an event (e.g., "it makes a loud noise"), (b) asked questions about or made statements regarding target actions of an event (while not simultaneously performing the target action; e.g., "put that [indicating the metal plate] on there [indicating the cross piece]"), or (c) requested or commented on an as yet unseen prop or event (e.g., "can I see the bell?").

2. Nonmnemonic utterances were propositional units judged to be relevant to the props or events but that did not indicate memory for the previous experience. They included narration of ongoing target actions (e.g., saying "hang it up" while placing the metal plate on the cross piece), conventional labels for objects or the actions performed with them (e.g., "it's a hammer [for the mallet used to hit the bell]," or, for the mallet, "you pound it"), general questions asked about the props or events (e.g., "what is this?"), comments or statements about nontarget activities (e.g., "we can make a fire station"), repetitions of the experimenter's or child's own verbalizations, and general requests or comments (e.g., "I want some more toys").[2]

Utterances that were not relevant to the props or events (e.g., "we have a kitty!") were considered to be off-task and were not considered further. Utterances judged to be unintelligible were coded as unclear and were not considered further.

A total of four coders (one of whom was Maria G. Kroupina) established reliability on the coding scheme. Working from the videotapes and transcripts, each individual coded a portion of the sessions, with the majority of coding conducted

---

[2]The coding scheme is based on Bauer, Kroupina, et al. (1998). In that study, utterances presently classified as nonmnemonic were differentiated into several more specific categories, including narration, labels for objects, labels for actions, and generic utterances (see Bauer, Kroupina, et al., 1998, for category descriptions). Although conceptually utterances falling into these categories might have indicated memory for the event sequences, empirically, none did (i.e., in no case did children produce more of these utterance types on events previously experienced relative to new event sequences). For that reason, they are appropriately considered to be nonmnemonic. In this study, we first classified all utterances into the more specific categories used in Bauer, Kroupina, et al. Once again, empirically, none of the categories yielded evidence of verbal memory for the events (details available from Patricia J. Bauer). In consideration of space constraints, we present the results only for the composite variable of all nonmemory related utterances.

by two of the coders. Propositions that were ambiguous as to their mnemonic status were discussed among the coders and classified after consensus was reached. Independent recoding of the transcriptions of 25% of the sessions by two of the coders yielded reliability in the range of 79% to 100% across the experiments. In Experiment 1, reliability of scoring was 93% for both delayed-recall test sessions (range = 83–99% and 79–97%, for Tests 1 and 2, respectively). In Experiment 2, reliability of scoring was 97% (range = 89–100%) and 93% (range = 90–97%) for delayed-recall Tests 1 and 2, respectively.

EXPERIMENT 1

The purpose of Experiment 1 was to determine whether children who had experienced a long delay (i.e., $M = 11$ months) between exposure and delayed-recall Test 1 spontaneously provided verbal reports about the events at that test, and whether verbal reports of the events could be elicited an average of 7 to 15 months later, at delayed-recall Test 2. Conducted on an independent sample drawn from the same parent study, the experiment affords a test for replication of the results of Bauer, Kroupina, et al. (1998). By including children who had been only 13 months of age at enrollment in the parent study, it also permits a strong test of the role of language at the time of encoding on later verbal accessibility: As a group, the youngest children were the least verbal at the time of encoding of the events.

Method

Participants. The participants were 36 children enrolled in the parent study at 13 months ($n = 12$), 16 months ($n = 12$), and 20 months ($n = 12$). Roughly one half of the children in each age group experienced a delay of 9 months and one half experienced a delay of 12 months between exposure to the test events and delayed-recall Test 1. The children were drawn from the longer delay conditions to test for replication of the results of Bauer, Kroupina, et al. (1998). Children were drawn from both the 9- and 12-month delay conditions to provide a sufficient number of participants. Descriptive statistics on the children's ages at enrollment and at each test, and on the lengths of the delays that they experienced, are provided in Table 1, Panel A.

Results

Delayed-recall Test 1 (9–12 months after initial exposure). Children's spontaneous verbal mnemonic and nonmnemonic behaviors were evaluated in separate 3 (age at enrollment: 13 months, 16 months, 20 months) × 3 (sequence type: enabling, mixed, arbitrary) × 3 (experience condition: imitated, watched, new) mixed analyses of variance (ANOVAs), with repeated measures on sequence type and experience condition (see Table 2, Panel A, for descriptive statistics). There was no evidence of verbal expression of memory: The number of utterances classified as mnemonic did not differ on events previously imitated, events previously only watched, and new events. Neither were there effects of experience condition in the category of nonmnemonic utterances. Thus, the number of utterances produced did not differ as a function of previous experience of the events.

There was a reliable effect of age on production of nonmnemonic utterances: $F(2, 33) = 7.22, p < .008$. The number of nonmnemonic utterances produced by the children who had been 13 and 16 months at enrollment did not differ, and both age groups produced fewer utterances than the children who had been 20 months at enrollment (Tukey, $p < .05$).

There were reliable effects of sequence type on production of both mnemonic and nonmnemonic utterances, $Fs(2, 66) = 3.67$ and $8.68, ps < .03$, respectively. In both cases, the number of utterances produced was greater for arbitrarily ordered events than for events constrained by enabling relations (Tukey, $p < .05$). The number of utterances about mixed events was intermediate, and either did not differ from the other two event types (mnemonic utterances), or was lower than the number produced about arbitrarily ordered events, but did not differ from enabling events (total nonmnemonic utterances).

Delayed-recall Test 2.   Whereas there was no evidence of spontaneous verbal mnemonic expression at delayed-recall Test 1, at delayed-recall Test 2, the children originally enrolled at 20 months provided evidence of verbally accessible memories. In contrast, the children originally enrolled at 13 and 16 months did not provide evidence of verbally accessible event memories, even though verbal reports were specifically elicited. Specifically, the numbers of mnemonic and nonmnemonic utterances that the children produced were analyzed in separate 3 (age at enrollment: 13 months, 16 months, 20 months) × 3 (sequence type: enabling, mixed, arbitrary) × 4 (experience condition: imitated, watched, new at delayed-recall Test 1, new at delayed-recall Test 2) × 2 (prop condition: before props, after props) mixed ANOVAs. For mnemonic utterances, main effects of experience condition and prop condition were qualified by the three-way interaction with age, $F(6, 99) = 2.20, p < .05$. Separate analyses by prop condition produced no effects once the props were given to the children. Indeed, once they had the props the children produced very few utterances classified as mnemonic ($M = 0.06, SD = 0.36$). That the number of utterances classified as mnemonic would be greater before versus after the props were provided, $F(1, 33) = 214.90, p < .001$, is to be expected, given the manner in which children's verbal behavior was scored: Whereas, once they had the props, the children could name or describe an event (coding subcategory "a"), they were unlikely to ask questions or make statements about target ac-

TABLE 2
Mean Number of Utterances Produced and Standard Deviations
in Experiments 1 and 2

	No. of Utterances Produced							
	Delayed-Recall Test 1				Delayed-Recall Test 2			
	Mnemonic		Nonmnemonic		Mnemonic		Nonmnemonic	
Experiment–Group	M	SD	M	SD	M	SD	M	SD
Panel A: Experiment 1								
13 month								
Imitate	0.03	0.17	5.59	5.29	1.31	1.26	10.33	7.05
Watch	0.03	0.17	5.16	4.34	1.04	0.94	13.16	9.52
New at Delay 1	0.06	0.23	4.22	3.29	1.50	1.28	10.83	6.50
New at Delay 2	na	—	na	—	1.05	0.92	9.41	6.37
16 month								
Imitate	0.17	0.70	6.40	5.29	1.61	1.32	11.92	7.01
Watch	0.03	0.17	6.64	6.25	1.75	1.42	12.44	6.77
New at Delay 1	0.06	0.23	5.06	4.47	1.00	1.24	14.54	9.59
New at Delay 2	na	—	na	—	1.36	1.22	13.17	9.38
20 month								
Imitate	0.06	0.23	9.44	5.86	2.17	1.56	12.01	7.66
Watch	0.22	0.54	11.06	5.66	2.28	1.50	13.28	7.89
New at Delay 1	0.19	0.52	11.94	6.64	1.58	1.32	13.19	7.58
New at Delay 2	na	—	na	—	1.19	1.12	13.81	8.62
Panel B: Experiment 2								
13 month								
Imitate	0.00	—	0.47	1.33	1.59	1.33	10.90	8.63
Watch	0.00	—	0.17	0.53	1.33	1.54	16.60	41.23
New at Delay 1	0.00	—	0.23	0.68	0.86	1.01	16.22	42.07
New at Delay 2	na	—	na	—	1.29	1.30	22.05	58.41
16 month								
Imitate	0.07	0.25	2.10	3.25	1.37	1.35	11.07	7.62
Watch	0.00	—	2.93	4.25	1.00	1.14	10.67	7.12
New at Delay 1	0.00	—	2.33	3.26	0.98	1.15	11.60	7.08
New at Delay 2	na	—	na	—	1.14	1.38	11.41	8.78
20 month								
Imitate	0.00	—	3.69	3.46	1.44	1.31	17.60	12.58
Watch	0.07	0.27	3.33	3.45	1.20	1.32	16.61	11.15
New at Delay 1	0.00	—	9.31	23.34	1.15	1.46	18.15	9.73
New at Delay 2	na	—	na	—	1.27	1.48	15.54	8.58

Note. Means reflect the number of utterances produced before the props were provided to the children. na = not applicable.

tions without also performing them (coding subcategory "b"), and they were unlikely to request or comment on another, as yet unseen, prop (coding subcategory "c"), while interacting with the one in front of them (see previous description of scoring).

Analysis of the children's verbal mnemonic behavior before the props were provided yielded an Age × Experience condition interaction: $F(6, 99) = 2.75$, $p < .02$. Separate analyses by age reveal no effects of experience condition for the two younger groups. For the children who had been 20 months at enrollment in the parent study, the effect of experience condition was reliable, $F(3, 33) = 5.16$, $p < .005$. Dunnett's tests, $p < .05$, reveal that the children produced a larger number of utterances classified as mnemonic on the events that they originally were permitted to imitate and on the events that they originally had only watched, relative to on the events that were new at delayed-recall Test 2. The number of utterances classified as mnemonic did not differ for the events that had been new at delayed-recall Test 1 and on the events that were new at delayed-recall Test 2. Thus, the oldest children provided evidence of verbal memory for the events to which they had been exposed at the age of 20 months and had re-experienced at delayed-recall Test 1, but not for the events that they experienced only once, at delayed-recall Test 1. There was no evidence of verbally accessible memories from the children who had been 13 and 16 months at the time of original exposure to the event sequences.

For mnemonic utterances, the main effect of sequence type was qualified by a Sequence type × Experience condition interaction, $F(6, 198) = 2.20$, $p < .05$. Analysis of the interaction by sequence type reveals no evidence of verbal expression of memory for the mixed events. For the arbitrarily ordered events, the main effect of experience condition, $F(3, 105) = 3.13$, $p < .03$, revealed larger numbers of mnemonic utterances on events originally imitated, events originally watched, and events new at delayed-recall Test 1, relative to events new at delayed-recall Test 2 ($Ms = 1.11$, 1.05, 1.07, and 0.68; $SDs = 1.63$, 1.50, 1.37, and 1.06, respectively). Thus, on the events about which the children had talked the most at the first delayed-recall test, they produced mnemonic utterances at the second delayed-recall test. For events constrained by enabling relations, it was only on event sequences originally watched that the children provided verbal evidence of memory at delayed-recall Test 2 ($Ms = 0.78$, 0.65, 0.40, and 0.46; $SDs = 1.18$, 1.06, 0.76, and 0.77, for watched, imitated, new at delayed-recall Test 1, and new at delayed-recall Test 2, respectively).

Verbal evidence of memory in the sample of children originally enrolled at 20 months of age and on arbitrarily ordered and enabling event sequences was not an artifact of greater overall talkativeness in these cells by the children at delayed-recall Test 2: Analysis of the children's nonmnemonic utterances produced no reliable effects. Thus, differential patterns of elicited verbal behavior as a function of age and sequence type were confined to mnemonic utterances.

TABLE 3
Mean Reported Productive Vocabulary Scores and Standard Deviations
of Children in Experiments 1 and 2

| | | Reported Productive Vocabulary Scores | | | |
| | | Enrollment | | Delayed-Recall Test 1 | |
Experiment–Group	n^a	M	SD	M	SD
Panel A: Experiment 1					
13 month	12/12	13.58	20.45	305.00	146.27
16 month	11/12	33.09	32.07	420.58	157.74
20 month	12/12	194.50	190.23	550.42	134.07
Panel B: Experiment 2					
13 month	10/6	9.30	8.51	20.83	19.81
16 month	10/10	31.20	26.91	94.40	62.64
20 month	9/8	198.67	230.06	231.63	191.30

[a]Numerals indicate the numbers of children for whom vocabulary data were available at the time of enrollment/at the time of delayed-recall Test 1.

Predicting verbal expression of memory.   We conducted correlational analyses to identify possible predictors of children's verbal behavior at each delayed-recall test. In the interest of space, only significant correlations are reported. At the first delayed-recall test, spontaneous verbal mnemonic expression[3] was related to (a) age at the time of test, $r = .34, p < .04$, and (b) concurrent verbal fluency, as measured by the total number of nonmnemonic utterances produced, $r = .32, p = .05$. Verbal mnemonic expression was not related to age at the time of enrollment, parental reports of productive vocabulary at enrollment, or parental reports of productive vocabulary at delayed-recall Test 1 (see Table 3, Panel A, for descriptive statistics on reported productive vocabularies at enrollment and delayed-recall Test 1). Thus, variables from the time of enrollment were largely unpredictive of verbal mnemonic expression at the first delayed-recall test. Instead, concurrent age and concurrent verbal fluency were predictive.

At the second delayed-recall test, there were no concurrent relations. Thus, in contrast to the first delayed-recall test, age at the time of the second delayed-recall test was not related to verbal mnemonic expression.

Although there were no concurrent relations at the second delayed-recall test, there were a number of cross-lag relations. Specifically, elicited verbal mnemonic expression at delayed-recall Test 2 was predicted by reported productive vocabulary at the first delayed-recall test, $r = .42, p < .02$, and by children's age at the first

---

[3]For purposes of analysis via correlation and regression, only utterances on which children could produce true mnemonic utterances—namely, events previously imitated and previously only watched—are included in the verbal mnemonic total.

delayed-recall test, $r = .45$, $p < .006$. In addition, verbal mnemonic expression at delayed-recall Test 2 was negatively related to the length of the delay between the two test sessions, $r = -.40$, $p < .02$. Together, the three variables accounted for 25% of the variance in children's verbal mnemonic expression at delayed-recall Test 2, $F(3, 32) = 3.59$, $p < .03$. The single strongest predictor was children's age at delayed-recall Test 1, $F(1, 34) = 8.83$, $p < .006$. When age at the first delayed-recall test was entered as the first step in the regression equation, neither children's reported productive vocabulary at delayed-recall Test 1 nor the delay between the test sessions accounted for additional unique variance. Unlike Bauer, Kroupina, et al. (1998), verbal mnemonic expression at delayed-recall Test 1 was not predictive of verbal mnemonic expression at delayed-recall Test 2.

Discussion

At the first delayed-recall test, which occurred an average of 11 months after exposure to the events, as a group, the children did not spontaneously provide verbal evidence of memory. The children who were oldest at enrollment, and thus were the oldest at the first delayed-recall test, produced more nonmnemonic utterances, relative to the children in the two younger groups. At the second delayed-recall test, which took place an average of 7 to 15 months from the first test, the oldest children provided verbal evidence of memory for the events to which they had been exposed at 20 months and had re-experienced at delayed-recall Test 1. They did not provide verbal evidence of memory for events experienced only once, at delayed-recall Test 1. There was no evidence of verbally accessible memories from the children 13 and 16 months of age at the time of original exposure to the events. Thus, the children who were older and who had talked more at the first delayed-recall test (i.e., the children who had been 20 months at enrollment) were the ones who at the second delayed-recall test provided verbal evidence of memory.

At delayed-recall Test 1, the children spontaneously produced both more mnemonic and more nonmnemonic utterances about the arbitrarily ordered events. At delayed-recall Test 2, evidence of verbal mnemonic expression was more readily elicited for arbitrarily ordered events; the children had talked about the arbitrary events more at delayed-recall Test 1. Given generally lower levels of nonverbal recall of the order of arbitrarily ordered events (e.g., Bauer, Hertsgaard, et al., 1998; Wenner & Bauer, 1999), the apparent facility that the children in this research had producing mnemonic utterances about just such events may seem puzzling. However, as noted in Bauer et al. (2000), although memory for the temporal order of arbitrarily ordered events typically is not impressive, memory for the individual actions of them consistently is high. Moreover, the arbitrarily ordered events had themes that were perhaps more familiar to the children and thus, were more easily described by them (e.g., building a house or feeding a bunny a carrot). This is in contrast to the enabling events, which made use of more unique, specialized objects and themes that likely were more difficult to encode linguistically (e.g., making a gong or a jumper).

In a replication of Bauer, Kroupina, et al. (1998), variables from the time of enrollment were largely unpredictive of verbal mnemonic expression at delayed-recall Test 1. Instead, concurrent age and concurrent verbal fluency were predictive of verbal mnemonic expression. In contrast to the first delayed-recall test, at which spontaneous production of mnemonic utterances was related to concurrent age, age at the second delayed-recall test was not related to elicited verbal mnemonic expression. Verbal mnemonic expression at delayed-recall Test 2 was predicted by (a) reported productive vocabulary at the first delayed-recall test, (b) children's age at the first delayed-recall test, and (c) the length of the delay between the two test sessions.

EXPERIMENT 2

The purpose of Experiment 2 was to determine whether children who had experienced a short delay (i.e., $M = 2$ months) between exposure and delayed-recall Test 1 were able to provide verbal reports about the events. This question is particularly interesting because the children who initially experienced short delays endured especially long delays between the first and the second delayed-recall tests (M delay of 19 months between tests vs. 11 months for children in Experiment 1). Thus, they provide a strong test of later verbal accessibility of early memories. Moreover, relative to the children in Experiment 1, for children who experienced short initial delays, the first delayed-recall test occurred when the children were younger and, on average, of lesser language proficiency. Conversely, for the children in the shorter delay conditions, the first delayed-recall test occurred at a time when, as measured nonverbally, memory representations were robust, relative to those of the children in the longer delay conditions (see Bauer et al., 2000, for details of nonverbal recall memory performance).

Method

Participants.   The participants were 29 children: 10 were enrolled in the parent study at 13 months, 10 were enrolled at 16 months, and 9 were enrolled at 20 months. Roughly one half of the children in each group experienced a delay of 1 month, and one half experienced a delay of 3 months between exposure to the test events and delayed-recall Test 1. Children were drawn from both the 1- and 3-month delay conditions to provide a sufficient number of participants. Descriptive statistics on the children's ages at enrollment and test, and on the lengths of the between-test delays, are presented in Table 1, Panel B.

Results

Delayed-recall Test 1 (1–3 months after initial exposure).   Descriptive statistics on children's verbal mnemonic and nonmnemonic behaviors are provided in Table 2, Panel B. The children produced very few utterances classified as mnemonic, as is apparent in the table. Indeed, the frequency of production of mnemonic utterances was so low as to preclude formal analysis of the data. In lieu of formal analysis, we simply note that the children who had been 13 months at the time of exposure to the events produced no utterances classified as mnemonic. In contrast, the children 16 and 20 months of age at the time of exposure produced a few mnemonic utterances on events that they had imitated (16-month-olds) or on events that they had only watched (20-month-olds); they produced no mnemonic utterances on new events. Thus, there was some slim evidence of verbal mnemonic expression by children 16 and 20 months at the time of initial experience.

As in Experiment 1, we evaluated children's nonmnemonic verbal behavior in a 3 (age at enrollment: 13 months, 16 months, 20 months) × 3 (sequence type: enabling, mixed, arbitrary) × 3 (experience condition: imitated, watched, new) mixed ANOVA, with repeated measures on sequence type and experience condition. As observed in Experiment 1, there was a reliable age effect on children's spontaneous production of nonmnemonic utterances, $F(2, 26) = 7.65, p < .03$. The number of utterances produced by the children who had been 20 months at exposure to the events was greater than the number produced by the children who had been only 13 months (Tukey, $p < .05$). The 16-month-olds did not differ from either age group. There were no other significant effects.

Delayed-recall Test 2.   We evaluated the numbers of mnemonic and nonmnemonic utterances that the children produced in separate 3 (age at enrollment: 13 months, 16 months, 20 months) × 3 (sequence type: enabling, mixed, arbitrary) × 4 (experience condition: imitated, watched, new at delayed-recall Test 1, new at delayed-recall Test 2) × 2 (prop condition: before props, after props) mixed ANOVAs. For mnemonic utterances, main effects of sequence type and prop condition were qualified by the three-way interaction with experience condition, $F(6, 151) = 2.88, p < .02$. Follow-up analyses revealed no effects once the props were given to the children. Indeed, as in Experiment 1, once the children had the props, they produced very few utterances classified as mnemonic ($M = 0.05, SD = 0.22$). The number of utterances classified as mnemonic was significantly greater before versus after the props were provided, $F(1, 26) = 66.61, p < .001$.

Analysis of the children's verbal mnemonic behavior before the props were provided yielded the interaction of Sequence Type × Experience condition, $F(6, 164) = 3.03, p < .008$. Separate analyses by sequence type revealed no verbal evidence of memory for the enabling and mixed events. In contrast, on arbitrarily ordered events, the children produced a larger number of utterances classified as mnemonic on events that they had imitated prior to the original delay ($M = 2.00$, $SD = 1.41$) and on events that they had only watched ($M = 1.90$, $SD = 1.54$), relative to on events new at delayed-recall Test 2 ($M = 1.18$, $SD = 1.42$; Dunnett, $p < .05$). The number of utterances classified as mnemonic did not differ on events that were new at delayed-recall Test 1 ($M = 1.01$, $SD = 1.41$) and new at delayed-recall Test 2. Thus, on arbitrarily ordered events that the children originally experienced and then re-experienced at the first delayed-recall test, there was evidence of later verbal accessibility of memory. On events experienced only once at the first delayed-recall test, there was no evidence of later verbal accessibility.

Analysis of children's nonmnemonic verbal behavior yielded no effects of sequence type. Thus, the differential patterns of verbal behavior across sequence type were confined to mnemonic utterances. The interaction of Age × Prop condition was significant, $F(6, 78) = 5.90$, $p < .0001$. Before the props were provided, children who had been 20 months at enrollment produced a larger number of nonmnemonic utterances, relative to children who had been 13 and 16 months at the time of enrollment; the number of nonmnemonic utterances produced by children enrolled at 13 and 16 months did not differ. Once the props were provided, there were no differences in production of nonmnemonic utterances. There were no other reliable effects.

Predicting verbal expression of memory.   At the first delayed-recall test, spontaneous verbal mnemonic expression was related to reported productive vocabulary at the time of enrollment, $r = .56$, $p < .002$ (see Table 3, Panel B, for descriptive statistics). However, the predictive relation was not specific: Reported productive vocabulary at enrollment also was related to production of utterances classified as nonmnemonic. There were no other significant relations. Thus, consistent with the results of Experiment 1, verbal mnemonic expression was not related to children's age at enrollment. However, unlike Experiment 1, neither was verbal mnemonic expression related to children's age at the time of the delayed-recall test.

At the second delayed-recall test, as in Experiment 1, there were no concurrent relations. In contrast to Experiment 1, in which there were a number of cross-lag relations, in this study, over the average 19-month delay between the two tests, there were no cross-lag relations. Thus, over the long delay in this experiment, neither reported productive vocabulary at the first delayed-recall test, children's age at the first delayed-recall test, nor the length of the delay between the two delayed-recall tests, was related to elicited verbal mnemonic expression at 3 years of age. As in Experiment 1, neither was verbal mnemonic expression at delayed-recall Test 1 predictive.

Discussion

At the first delayed-recall test, which occurred an average of 2 months after initial exposure to the events, the children provided few mnemonic expressions. In fact, likely due to their young age and limited vocabularies, the children who had been only 13 months at the time of enrollment (and were, on average, only 14½ months old at the time of test), provided no utterances classified as mnemonic. The children in the two older age groups who were, on average, 18 and 22 months of age at the time of the test, provided very few mnemonic utterances. Nevertheless, those they did provide were in response to event sequences to which they previously had been exposed, rather than to sequences new to them. The only predictor of verbal mnemonic expression at the first test—namely, reported productive vocabulary at the time of enrollment—was not specific: It also related to children's production of nonmnemonic utterances.

At the second delayed-recall test, although the children did not provide verbal evidence of memory for the enabling or mixed sequences, they provided verbal mnemonic expressions about the arbitrarily ordered events. As in Experiment 1, verbal evidence of memory was apparent only on the events in which the children had prior experience; it was not apparent on the events they had experienced only once, at delayed-recall Test 1. That there was any evidence of verbal mnemonic expression is striking in light of the average 19-month delay over which it was apparent. The finding suggests that at least under certain, highly contextualized, circumstances, early memories are verbally accessible over the long term. Over the long delay, no variables from prior sessions were predictive of verbal mnemonic expression at delayed-recall Test 2.

GENERAL DISCUSSION

In Katherine Nelson's (e.g., 1993) social-construction model, autobiographical memory depends on a narrative structure within which events are organized and interpreted. As Nelson and her colleagues (e.g., Tessler & Nelson, 1994) illustrated, narrative organization is constructed over the preschool years, in the context of reminiscing with more seasoned practitioners (e.g., parents). Events experienced after the autobiographical system is underway can be encoded with reference to it. By default, events experienced prior to the construction of the system are not a part of it. They may become part of the system only if and when they are assimilated into the narrative format. Unfortunately, from the standpoint of later access to early life events, past events rarely are available for assimilation because (a) the events are, by definition, over, and (b) in young children, verbal cues such as are available in the context of conversations, are not particularly effective at reinstating memories. However, as observed over 20 years ago (Nelson & Ross, 1980), physical cues sometimes are effective at reinstating early memories. The results of the research presented here make clear that when strong physical cues and sufficient language skills are simultaneously present, children are able to use language to talk about the past. What is more, memories are verbally accessible even after long delays.

In Experiment 2 of this research, when tested roughly 2 months after experience of specific laboratory events, children who were the youngest at the time of experience, and thus youngest at the time of test, provided no verbal evidence of memory. Children who were 16 and 20 months of age at experience, and 17 to 23 months of age at test, provided only a few verbal mnemonic expressions. Although the children in Experiment 1 were, on average, older than the children in Experiment 2 at the time of the first delayed-recall test (which occurred on average, 11 months after experience of the events), they did not provide verbal evidence of memory. This finding stands in contrast to that of Bauer, Kroupina, et al. (1998). The discrepancy may in part be due to inclusion in this sample of children 13 months of age at the time of experience, whereas in Bauer, Kroupina, et al., only 16- and 20-month-olds were included. When tested nonverbally, after 9 and 12 months, the 13-month-olds no longer evidenced event memory (Bauer et al., 2000). It is highly unlikely then that they would evidence memory verbally. In addition, in Bauer, Kroupina, et al., the children were drawn from the 6- and 12-month delay conditions, whereas in this experiment, they were drawn from the 9- and 12-month delay conditions. As described in Bauer et al. (2000), performance by children in the 9-month delay condition was lower, relative to that of children in (a) the 6-month delay condition and, inexplicably, (b) the 12-month delay condition. Inclusion of children with lower levels of event memory as evidenced nonverbally may have resulted in lower levels of verbal recall as well. Contrary to expectations derived from Peterson and Rideout (1998), but consistent with Bauer, Kroupina, et al. (1998), variables from the time of enrollment did not predict verbal mnemonic expression. Rather, verbal mnemonic expression was predicted by concurrent age and concurrent verbal fluency.

As summarized in Experiment 1, the children who were the oldest at enrollment, and thus were the oldest at the first delayed-recall test, talked more during the first recall test session, relative to the children in the younger age groups. This apparently was crucial to later verbal accessibility of early memories: When they were tested an average of 7 to 15 months later, only the oldest children provided verbal evidence of memory for the events; the children who had been 13 and 16 months at the time of original exposure to the events did not evidence memory verbally. The absence of later verbal accessibility of memory by children younger than 20 months at enrollment seems to be reliable: In addition to this research,[4] it was apparent in Bauer, Kroupina, et al. (1998). Moreover, the pattern is reminiscent of that observed in Peterson and Rideout (1998), in which children who had been 13 to 18 months of age at the time of emergency services were unable to provide verbal accounts of their experiences, even once they acquired the necessary

---

[4]In addition to Experiment 1 of this research, failure of children enrolled at 16 months of age to provide evidence of later verbal access to early memories also was observed in the context of evaluation of verbal behavior as a function of test by the same experimenter versus a different experimenter (see Footnote 1; details are available from Patricia J. Bauer).

language skills. In contrast, children who had been 20 months and older at the time of their experiences were able to talk about them several months later.

Seemingly qualitative differences in the later accessibility of memories encoded before versus after 20 months of age, as assessed verbally, stands in contrast to the pattern of qualitative similarities when children's memories are tested nonverbally. Specifically, when they are tested using elicited and deferred imitation, the mnemonic behaviors of 13-, 16-, and 20-month-olds are determined by the same factors (e.g., the temporal structure of events, verbal reminders of the events; Bauer et al., 2000); children 16 and 20 months evidence memory over the same delays (Bauer et al., 2000; see also Meltzoff, 1995; see Bauer, in press-a, for a review). Given apparent similarities in the *nonverbal* memory representations of children who first experienced events at 20 months and children who experienced events when they were younger than 20 months, why might patterns of *verbal* expression of memory look so different for children of these ages? One possibility lies in the strengths of the memory representations formed by the children on each side of the apparent divide. For example, although in Bauer et al., both younger and older children evidenced memory over long delays: (a) 20-month-olds showed more robust initial learning of the events, and (b) even with differences in initial learning controlled, 20-month-olds exhibited higher levels of delayed recall, relative to 16-month-olds. Quantitative differences in the strengths of memory representations may have contributed to qualitative differences in verbal mnemonic expression. If this is the case, then we should find that variation in the strength of initial encoding (e.g., as a function of number of experiences of to-be-remembered events) relates systematically to subsequent verbal expression of memory.

An alternative possibility is that there is a minimum age or level of verbal competence that is required for later verbal accessibility of early memories. Support for this possibility would come in the form of findings that children younger than the threshold age or children with levels of verbal competence below the threshold (or both), are not able to verbally describe early memories, regardless of the adequacy with which the events initially were encoded. In the context of this research, it is noteworthy that at the time of enrollment, the average reported productive vocabularies of the 16-month-olds were below 50 words, whereas those of the 20-month-olds approached 200 words (see Table 3). A possible "threshold" level of linguistic competence could be anywhere between 50 and 200 words. With this suggestion we do not mean to imply that the 20-month-olds had such high levels of language competence that they represented the events primarily verbally. More likely, their levels of language proficiency were just high enough to provide linguistic "hooks" on which they later were able to hang further linguistic embellishments of their memory representations. With their lower levels of vocabulary, the children younger than 20 months may simply have lacked the requisite minimum language skills.

Whereas in Experiment 1, age at initial encoding of the event sequences proved to be an important determinant of later verbal memory, age at reexperience also emerged as an important variable. Indeed, the single strongest predictor of verbal mnemonic expression at age 3 years was children's ages at the first test. Children's language skills at the first test (which of course were correlated with age) also predicted verbal mnemonic expression at age 3. In addition, evidence of verbal mnemonic expression was more readily apparent on arbitrarily ordered events; the children had talked about the arbitrarily ordered events more at the first delayed-recall test.

In contrast to Experiment 1, in Experiment 2, neither age nor language at re-experience was related to elicited verbal mnemonic expression at age 3 years. There are three possible reasons for this difference across experiments. First, due to the younger ages of the children at re-experience, the sample as a whole was less verbally fluent. The oldest children in Experiment 2 had reported productive vocabularies that were smaller than those of the youngest children in Experiment 1 ($Ms =$ 231 and 305 words, respectively; see Table 3). Second, the delay between test sessions was longer in Experiment 2 ($M = 19$ months) than in Experiment 1 ($M = 11$ months); variables lose their predictive utility over time. Third, in Experiment 2, verbal mnemonic expression was not readily observed at age 3: The children provided verbal evidence of memory for the arbitrarily ordered events only. On reflection, that there was any verbal evidence of memory across an average delay of 16 to 23 months is striking. It suggests that at least under certain, highly contextualized circumstances, early memories are verbally accessible over the long term.

Together, the results of this research make clear that at least under some, highly contextualized conditions, children later can verbally access their early memories. Spontaneous verbal expression of memory at 14 to 31 months of age is determined primarily by concurrent age and concurrent verbal fluency (see also Bauer, Kroupina, et al., 1998). In turn, the number of verbal mnemonic expressions that can be elicited at age 3 seems to be determined by age and verbal fluency at the time of re-experience of events. Re-experience is particularly effective for children whose original exposure to events was at the age of 20 months of age.

It is important to note that it is events first experienced at 20 months of age, and then re-experienced at a later age and concomitant level of verbal fluency, that are verbally accessible at age 3. That is, under the circumstances of this research, the children did not provide verbal evidence of memory for events first encountered at delayed-recall Test 1. Thus, the effect seems to be one of initial experience at roughly 20 months, with subsequent re-experience at a time of greater availability of language. Children who at first experience were 20 months of age apparently formed event representations of adequate strength or had reached a level of linguistic competence sufficient to permit event-related verbal expression at the first delayed-recall test. At re-experience, the children were old enough, and thus, sufficiently linguistically competent, to augment their largely nonverbal memory representations with language and as a result, were able to talk about the events at age 3. Children who were younger at the time of re-experience, and thus less mnemonically or linguistically competent (or both), were not. The one exception to this pattern was arbitrarily ordered events that, due to their nature and design, may have lent themselves to description with more limited language (i.e., as discussed earlier, the arbitrarily ordered events had themes that were perhaps more familiar to the children and thus, were more easily described by them). Critically, this option too was dependent on prior experience of the events: Higher levels of production of utterances classified as mnemonic did not extend to arbitrarily ordered events with which the children had no previous experience (i.e., events new at delayed-recall Test 2) or had only one previous experience (i.e., events new at delayed-recall Test 1).

Why might it be the case that re-experience, but not necessarily first experience, of an event at a later age and concomitant level of language ability would be so crucial to later verbal accessibility of event memory? It is clear that children of the age of those in this research are able to talk about events experienced only once. For example, in Peterson and Rideout (1998), children who had been 26 months at the time of a trip to the emergency room were able to talk about the event months later. The children in Experiment 1 of this research were an average of 27 months at the time they experienced the new events at delayed-recall Test 1. This implies that it is not simply that the new events were experienced only once and the events to which the children had been exposed at enrollment were experienced multiple times. Rather, it seems that it was the act of retrieval of the memory for the original event that supported verbal accessibility in the 4th year of life. We suggest that at the time of retrieval, newly available language became integrated with the primarily nonverbal event representations, thereby strengthening the memory traces (for discussions of reintegration effects associated with memory reinstatement see, e.g., Howe, Courage, & Bryant-Brown, 1993; Hudson & Sheffield, 1998). Although we believe this the most likely explanation for the pattern obtained, we acknowledge that the design of these experiments precludes a definitive answer to the question. In ongoing research we are testing whether re-experience of events is necessary to ensure later verbal accessibility, or whether supporting retrieval by providing cues or reminders in the form of event-related props, without re-exposure to the modeled sequences, also permits long-term verbal accessibility.

To say that children's early memories later are "verbally accessible" does not imply that they are expressed or even encoded in narrative form. That is, the children in this research did not provide extended narratives about the events; we have no reason to believe that they possessed them. Rather, their mnemonic utterances were brief and to the point, for example, the name of an event or its outcome (e.g., "it makes a loud noise"). At the tender ages at which they were tested, children are only beginning to be reliable partners in conversations about past events; they are not yet competent independent story tellers. Indeed, we are suggesting that it is only because of the heavy contextual support available to them that the children produced any mnemonic verbalizations. In Nelson's (1996) terms, these verbalizations would be considered mimetic: They are tied to the concrete actions and sequences with which they are associated (see Tomasello, 2001/this issue, for discussion of some of the implications of this aspect of Nelson's perspective). These early mnemonic verbalizations are significant nonetheless because of their status as potential "bridges" between the preverbal past and the verbal present. Under typical circumstances, memories from early in life do not make the crossing because by the time the narrative skills necessary to talk about the past are available, the experiences are long since forgotten. Because language is not a particularly effective means of retrieval for pre- and early-verbal memories, even if linguistic reminders are provided, they are not effective. However, in circumstances such as this research, in which strong physical cues are available, the memories can be retrieved. Once retrieved, children can use their newly developed language skills to augment their primarily nonverbal representations with language.

How do these findings bear on Katherine Nelson's (1993) theory of autobiographical memory development? We do not claim that because the children in this research provided some verbal tokens about the events of making gongs and jumpers, they had autobiographical memories of the events. Instead, our argument is that early memories are not, by definition, "ineligible" for inclusion in autobiography. They are not typically seen there not because they were not originally encoded in the narrative form that Nelson (1993) associated with autobiography, but because they do not typically get assimilated to it once it is available. One implication of this research is that there are circumstances under which the necessary assimilative conditions can be met and early memories made candidates for inclusion in autobiography. In the same breath, we readily acknowledge that memories of making gongs and jumpers are not good candidates for autobiography for another reason: They are not particularly personally significant events. However, under the circumstances of this research, had the events that the children experienced been more personally meaningful, they may well have wound up as part of autobiography. That perhaps not the events themselves, but the experience of the laboratory, may make it into autobiography is supported by spontaneous comments by some of the participants in this research who even now, at 6½ to 9 years of age, are returning to the laboratory for interviews about some of their early experiences. Although we can offer no quantification at this time, we note that many of the children have commented on their recollections of coming to the laboratory and "playing with toys" when they were very young.

ACKNOWLEDGMENTS

This research was supported by a McKnight-Land Grant professorship, a grant from the Graduate School of the University of Minnesota, and the National Institute of Child Health and Human Development Grant HD–28425.

We thank Patricia Dropik and Sandi Wewerka for assisting with data collection; Christopher Stevens for expert coding of the children's verbalizations; Emily Stark for her invaluable assistance with data management and analysis; Jennifer Rademacher and Jennie Waters, and many other members of the Cognition in the Transition laboratory group, for their help in data collection, transcription, and management; and Robyn Fivush, Judith Hudson, and Joan Lucariello for their invitation to contribute to this special issue. We extend a special message of gratitude to the children and parents whose dedication to the effort made this work possible.

REFERENCES

Bauer, P. J. (in press-a). Early memory development. In U. Goswami (Ed.), *Handbook of cognitive development. Oxford, England: Blackwell.*

Bauer, P. J. (in press-b). New developments in the study of infant memory. In D. M. Teti (Ed.), *Handbook of research methods in developmental psychology.* Oxford, England: Blackwell.

Bauer, P. J., & Dow, G. A. A. (1994). Episodic memory in 16- and 20-month-old children: Specifics are generalized, but not forgotten. *Developmental Psychology, 30,* 403–417.

Bauer, P. J., Hertsgaard, L. A., Dropik, P., & Daly, B. P. (1998). When even arbitrary order becomes important: Developments in reliable temporal sequencing of arbitrarily ordered events. *Memory, 6,* 165–198.

Bauer, P. J., Hertsgaard, L. A., & Wewerka, S. S. (1995). Effects of experience and reminding on long-term recall in infancy: Remembering not to forget. *Journal of Experimental Child Psychology, 59,* 260–298.

Bauer, P. J., Kroupina, M. G., Schwade, J. A., Dropik, P., & Wewerka, S. S. (1998). If memory serves, will language? Later verbal accessibility of early memories. *Development and Psychopathology, 10,* 655–679.

Bauer, P. J., Wenner, J. A., Dropik, P. L., & Wewerka, S. S. (2000). Parameters of remembering and forgetting in the transition from infancy to early childhood. *Monographs of the Society for Research in Child Development, 65*(4, Serial No. 263).

Bauer, P. J., & Wewerka, S. S. (1995). One- to two-year-olds' recall of events: The more expressed, the more impressed. *Journal of Experimental Child Psychology, 59,* 475–496.

Bauer, P. J., & Wewerka, S. S. (1997). Saying is revealing: Verbal expression of event memory in the transition from infancy to early childhood. In P. van den Broek, P. J. Bauer, & T. Bourg (Eds.), *Developmental spans in event comprehension and representation: Bridging fictional and actual events* (pp. 139–168). Mahwah, NJ: Lawrence Erlbaum Associates, Inc.

Bauer, P. J., Wiebe, S., Waters, J. M., & Bangston, S. K. (2001). Reexposure breeds recall: Effects of experience on 9-month-olds' ordered recall. *Journal of Experimental Child Psychology, 80,* 174–200.

Carver, L. J., & Bauer, P. J. (1999). When the event is more than the sum of its parts: Nine-month-olds' long-term ordered recall. *Memory, 7,* 147–174.

Carver, L. J., & Bauer, P. J. (in press). The dawning of a past: The emergence of long-term explicit memory in infancy. *Journal of Experimental Psychology: General.*

Fenson, L., Dale, P. S., Reznick, J. S., Bates, E., Thal, D. J., & Pethick, S. J. (1994). Variability in early communicative development. *Monographs of the Society for Research in Child Development, 59*(5, Serial No. 242).

Fivush, R., Gray, J. T., & Fromhoff, F. A. (1987). Two-year-olds talk about the past. *Cognitive Development, 2,* 393–410.

Hamond, N. R., & Fivush, R. (1991). Memories of Mickey Mouse: Young children recount their trip to Disney World. *Cognitive Development, 6,* 433–448.

Howe, M. L., Courage, M. L., & Bryant-Brown, L. (1993). Reinstating preschoolers' memories. *Developmental Psychology, 29,* 854–869.

Hudson, J. A. (1993). Reminiscing with mothers and others: Autobiographical memory in young two-year-olds. *Journal of Narrative and Life History, 3,* 1–32.

Hudson, J. A., & Sheffield, E.G. (1998). Déjà vu all over again: Effects of reenactment on toddlers' event memory. *Child Development, 69,* 51–67.

Lechuga, M. T., Marcos-Ruiz, R., & Bauer, P. J. (2001). Episodic recall of specifics and generalization coexist in 25-month-old children. *Memory, 9,* 117–132.

Meltzoff, A. N. (1995). What infant memory tells us about infantile amnesia: Long-term recall and deferred imitation. *Journal of Experimental Child Psychology, 59,* 497–515.

Myers, N. A., Clifton, R. K., & Clarkson, M. G. (1987). When they were very young: Almost-threes remember two years ago. *Infant Behavior and Development, 10,* 123–132.

Nelson, K. (Ed.). (1986). *Event knowledge: Structure and function in development.* Hillsdale, NJ: Lawrence Erlbaum Associates, Inc.

Nelson, K. (Ed.). (1989). *Narratives from the crib.* Cambridge, MA: Harvard University Press.

Nelson, K. (1993). The psychological and social origins of autobiographical memory. *Psychological Science, 4,* 1–8.

Nelson, K. (1996). *Language in cognitive development: The emergence of the mediated mind.* New York: Cambridge University Press.

Nelson, K., & Gruendel, J. (1981). Generalized event representations: Basic building blocks of cognitive development. In M. E. Lamb & A. L. Brown (Eds.), *Advances in developmental psychology* (Vol. 1, pp. 131–158). Hillsdale, NJ: Lawrence Erlbaum Associates, Inc.

Nelson, K., & Gruendel, J. (1986). Children's scripts. In K. Nelson (Ed.), *Event knowledge: Structure and function in development* (pp. 21–46). Hillsdale, NJ: Lawrence Erlbaum Associates, Inc.

Nelson, K., & Ross, G. (1980). The generalities and specifics of long-term memory in infants and young children. In M. Perlmutter (Ed.), *New directions for child development: Children's memory* (pp. 87–101). San Francisco: Jossey-Bass.

Peterson, C., & Rideout, R. (1998). Memory for medical emergencies experienced by 1- and 2-year-olds. *Developmental Psychology, 34,* 1059–1072.

Ratner, H. H. (1980). The role of social context in memory development. In M. Perlmutter (Ed.), *New directions for child development: Children's memory* (pp. 49–67). San Francisco: Jossey-Bass.

Tessler, M., & Nelson, K. (1994). Making memories: The influence of joint encoding on later recall. *Consciousness and Cognition, 3,* 307–326.

Todd, C. M., & Perlmutter, M. (1980). Reality recalled by preschool children. In M. Perlmutter (Ed.), *New directions for child development: Children's memory* (pp. 69–85). San Francisco: Jossey-Bass.

Wenner, J. A., & Bauer, P. J. (1999). Bringing order to the arbitrary: One- to two-year-olds' recall of event sequences. *Infant Behavior and Development, 22,* 585–590.

JOURNAL OF COGNITION AND DEVELOPMENT, 3(1), 49–71
Copyright © 2002, Lawrence Erlbaum Associates, Inc.

"Do You Know What We're Going to Do This Summer?": Mothers' Talk to Preschool Children About Future Events

Judith A. Hudson

Department of Psychology
Rutgers, The State University of New Jersey

Mothers engaged their 2½- and 4-year-old children in conversations about novel and familiar past and future events. Analyses focused on (a) evidence for style differences in mothers' elicitation of future event talk, (b) the temporal frames of references (past, future, general, and hypothetical) mothers used across conversations, and (c) mothers' use of conventional time terms (e.g., last week, on Sunday). Mothers showed little consistency in style of elicitation over past and future conversations. In conversations about future events, mothers produced more references to future time, more hypothetical references, and more conventional time references. In talking about the past, mothers referred to the past more often and used more sequence terms. Mothers also varied their temporal references when talking about novel and familiar events. Results are discussed in terms of how conversations about future events can contribute to the development of children's concepts of time.

Katherine Nelson (1986, 1993, 1996) long maintained that a critical function of early memory development is the prediction of future events. Young children form generalized event representations of recurring events and retain episodic memories of individual event episodes to understand and predict future everyday occurrences. For example, a 3-year-old child who has acquired a general event representation of the sequence of actions involved in going to day care can anticipate when (in the event sequence) snacks and play time will occur as well as when his or her mother or father will return. He or she might also speculate as to the probability of eating bananas or crackers for snack on a given day, based on past regularities in the menu. Therefore, the early development of event memory is future driven in

---

Requests for reprints should be sent to Judith A. Hudson, Department of Psychology, Rutgers, The State University of New Jersey, 53 Avenue E, Piscataway, NJ 08854. E-mail: jhudson@rci.rutgers.edu

that the memory representations serve the function of anticipating the future. Only later, sometime after the age of 3 years, do children begin to understand the value of remembering for remembering's sake; that is, the autobiographic function of event memories. According to the social interactionist perspective, the development of autobiographic memory occurs through conversations about past events with adult partners (Fivush, 1997; Hudson, 1990; Nelson, 1993, 1996). As parents engage their children in talk about "what happened when," children learn how to talk about their memories with others and understand the value of sharing memory information with a conversational partner.

Despite the early and continued importance of event knowledge for predicting future events, relatively little research has focused on children's conceptualization of future events. However, conversations about the future may be just as important for young children to develop an explicit concept of future time as conversations about past events are for the development of autobiographic memory. Nelson (1996) argued that verbal social interactions are critical contexts for the development of time concepts. Preliminary concepts of sequence and reoccurrence may be grasped by very young, preverbal children, but to understand conventional time systems, children must learn how these fundamental time concepts are coordinated and quantified in language. For example, knowing what happens when you go to the playground and knowing that you go there frequently involves understanding the temporal concepts of sequence and reoccurrence, but knowing that one goes to the playground every Saturday involves understanding how reoccurrence is represented in the conventional units of days and weeks. Knowing that you go to the pool when it is warm outside places an event within a sequence of changing seasons; knowing that you go to the pool in summer involves coordinating that sequence into conventional concepts of seasons and annual cycles. Verbal discussions are critical for the development of conventional time concepts because conventional time concepts must be acquired through language. According to Nelson (1996), the concept of time is itself a social construction and it is conveyed to children through language:

> The child alone cannot *discover* time, because (unlike concrete objects) it is not an entity that exits to be discovered. Rather, conceptions of process and change have led different societies to conceptualize time in different ways, and those ways are conveyed to children through language forms. (p. 288)

Although language and social interaction are thought to play a central role in the development of children's understanding of time, few investigations have examined how natural conversations about everyday events contribute to children's conceptualizations of time. Most of the research on children's temporal understanding has focused on nonverbal assessments. Using measures of behavioral enactment of ordered event sequences, there is ample evidence that during the first 2 years of life, children are able to learn simple temporal sequences and anticipate "what happens next" (e.g., Bauer, 1995). Using picture-sequencing tasks, research has shown that children develop a more complex understanding of the temporal structure of real-world events during the ages of 3 to 8 years (Benson, 1997; Friedman, 1977, 1986, 1990, 1991; Friedman & Brudos, 1988). Friedman conducted extensive research into children's representations of temporal structure using picture-sequencing tasks in which children are asked to order events along a time line relative to the present time or to a designated point within a sequence (e.g., breakfast). This line of research indicated that by 4 to 5 years of age, children in the United States can represent the temporal sequence of the main events in their day (Friedman, 1977, 1990, 1992; Friedman & Brudos, 1988), by 6 to 7 years they can order seasonal events (Friedman, 1977, 1990), and by 7 to 8 years they can correctly order cards listing the days in the week and months in the year (Friedman, 1977, 1986).

Friedman (1989, 1990, 1992) proposed that preschool children develop a spatially organized image representation of daily activities including information about both sequence and the magnitude of intervals separating event elements. Four-year-olds use this spatial image to locate past events relative to the present and accurately judge how long ago birthdays and holidays occurred (Friedman & Kemp 1998). Although children can also use this spatial image to represent future time and judge the distances of future events, 4-year-olds are less successful in judging future than past events (Friedman, 2000).

Benson (1997) also used a picture-sequencing task to test whether 4- and 5-year-olds could correctly sequence 12 daily activities from the past (yesterday), present (today), and future (tomorrow) along a time line. Children at both ages correctly sequenced these activities, although they were more accurate in sequencing activities from the past than from the future. These findings provide further evidence that preschool children's concepts of past and future events develop in the context of thinking about routine events and that thinking about the future may be more difficult for young children than thinking about the past.

Research that has investigated children's understanding and use of temporal language has focused on children's acquisition of grammatical markers (tense, modality, and aspect) and lexical markers such as adverbs ("tomorrow," "later"), prepositions ("on Monday," "after"), and conjunctions ("and then"), examining both spontaneous speech and speech used in experimental situations. There is general agreement that by the age of 2 years, children can differentiate between past, present, and future reference using both tense and aspect (Harner, 1981; Nelson, 1993; Sachs, 1983). An understanding of "before" and "after" as well as more complex conventional time terminology ("tomorrow," "next week") is achieved during the years 4 to 7 (see Benson, 1997, for a review).

Although several studies have used children's spontaneous productions as the basis for the analysis of children's understanding of temporal terms (e.g., Harner, 1981; Sachs, 1983), these investigations did not examine how the temporal language used within conversations maps onto actual past, present, and future events or how an overall narrative of a past or future event is co-constructed. These types of analysis are crucial for understanding how children learn to coordinate memories of past events and general event knowledge about the regular sequence of recurring events into a mental time line. Nelson (1996) and Friedman (1990, 1992) proposed that both the regularity of the sequencing of routine events in the real world and social interactions between parent and child that accompany these events provide the basis for young children's understanding of temporal relations. Extended conversations with parents may assist young children in coordinating time concepts and language forms by providing an extended narrative context in which the relations between actual event time and linguistic forms for referencing time are understood. Before children are able to coordinate event memories, general event knowledge, and speculations about the future into coherent verbal forms with appropriate temporal markers, they may be able to provide appropriate event information as queried by parents while co-constructing narratives about past and future events. Conversations about both the past and the future may be important contexts for children to understand how event sequences and temporal concepts are related in language and thought.

Research on how parents talk about the past has made significant strides in examining the structure and content of parent–child memory conversations. Consistent with Vygotsky's (1978) theory of the role of social interaction in cognitive development, this line of research suggests that through conversations about past events, parents are teaching their children the social significance of sharing memories, and they are also assisting children in development of the memory and narrative skills necessary for remembering and talking about the past. This line of research has also shown that variations in how parents engage their children in past talk can affect children's ability to narrate independent memory accounts. In particular, two styles of elicitation have been identified (Engel, 1986; Fivush & Fromhoff, 1988; Hudson, 1990; McCabe & Peterson, 1991; Reese & Fivush, 1993). Parents using an *elaborative* style tend to pose many questions to their children, and they provide more and more information in their repeated queries. Parents using an elaborative style also provide information about their own recollections and elaborate on their children's responses even if children's answers do not directly answer the questions that were posed. Parents using a *repetitive* style tend to repeat very similar questions without necessarily providing additional information. Longitudinal research has indicated that children of parents who use an elaborative style are more elaborative in their own personal narrative reports over time (McCabe & Peterson, 1991; Reese, Haden, & Fivush, 1993).

Investigations of parent–child conversations about future are rare, but two studies have examined the frequency of talk about the past and future in everyday parent–child interactions. Lucariello and Nelson (1987) examined the temporal language mothers used while talking with 2-year-old children in three event contexts: during a routine event, during unstructured free play, and during thematic play. The rates of talk about the past and future were very similar, but both past and future talk were more frequent in the routine event contexts than either of the play contexts, suggesting that shared event knowledge facilitated temporally displaced language use. Benson, Talmi, and Haith (1999) examined parental time talk in 16 parent–child dyads when the children were 14, 20, and 32 months old using data from the Child Language Data Exchange System (CHILDES; MacWhinney, 1995). Parental time talk, that is, utterances that included a temporal reference, increased from 37% of the total number of utterances directed to children at 14 months to 52% at 32 months. Although more of adult utterances referred to current events (31%), reference to future events (14%) was significantly greater than reference to past events (3%). Interestingly, the percentage of parental talk about the past remained relatively constant at 2% to 3%, but the percentage of parental talk about the future increased from 11% at 14 months to 16% at 32 months.

These investigations provided evidence that parents talk to young children about future events at least as much as they talk about the past and perhaps even more often. Therefore, it is possible that how parents talk about the future can affect the development of children's understanding of future time. However, these investigations only studied children up to 32 months of age. We know little about how parents talk with older children about the future and how future talk affects the development of children's time concepts. In addition, these investigations focused on the amount of talk about the future that is directed toward young children, but not the content. To understand how conversations about the future contribute to young children's conceptualizations of future time, we need to examine the content of parent and child future talk. Verbal discussion about future events may be especially important for the development of future time concepts because the future is essentially a hypothetical construct. In discussions of the past, parents and children can access their own memories and discuss that information with their partner. Although memories of past events and general event knowledge may contribute to the discussion of future events, the resulting conversation must be speculative as participants discuss what could or probably will occur.

This investigation examines how mothers engage young children in talk about the past and future in naturalistic conversations. Special attention is focused on discussion of future events because less is known about how future events are talked about in a conversational format. Mothers of 2½- and 4-year-old children were asked to initiate conversations with their children about both past and future events. These age groups were selected for several reasons. Maternal style differences in past talk are apparent in mothers of children from 24 to 30 months of age (Farrant & Reese, 2000; Hudson, 1990, 1993), so the younger age group represented an early point at which maternal style differences might also be apparent in future talk. Several studies have found consistent style differences in maternal elicitation style in preschool children from 3 to 5 years of age that influence children's participation (Fivush & Fromhoff, 1988; Reese et al., 1993). Therefore, the

4-year-old age group included in this investigation provided a comparison group at an age at which children contribute more to conversations and may be more affected by maternal style differences.

These data were used to address several questions. First, we examined the stability of maternal styles over two elicitation contexts. On the one hand, mothers may use the same type of style across contexts, indicating that these styles reflect general stylistic differences in how mothers interact verbally with their preschool children. On the other hand, parents' styles may vary across contexts, indicating that these styles are task dependent and that parents use different styles depending on the goals of the interaction. Research on maternal reminiscing styles has found evidence for stability in style over time (Reese et al., 1993) and across children in the same family (Haden, 1998). However, Haden and Fivush (1996) found that reminiscing style did not generalize to other conversational contexts such as free play. The past elicitation context may have been more task oriented than the play context and parents may have been more willing to let their children take the lead in the play context. In eliciting past and future talk, parents may be more likely to view themselves as the leader across both tasks. Comparing elicitation styles across the two contexts can provide data on whether parents use similar or different styles to elicit verbal information about past and future events from children.

Second, do mothers engage preschool children in planning for future events, or do they simply tell them what will happen? To engage children in verbal discussion about an unknown future, mothers may ask children to speculate about what might happen and discuss children's preferences, especially if parents believe that children have a knowledge base from which to make predictions. To examine whether mothers are more likely to engage children in speculative thinking about future events if they believe their children have some knowledge, mothers were asked to discuss both novel events (never experienced or experienced only once) and familiar events (experienced two or more times) in past and future conversations.

Finally, we examined the temporal terms that parents used when talking to their children about past and future events. Because research has shown that children younger than 4 years old have a limited understanding of conventional time language, it was expected that mothers would use less-conventional time language with younger children. Mothers may also vary in the frequency of temporal language use across past and future conversations.

METHOD

Participants

Fifty-six children and their mothers participated in the study including twenty-eight 2½-year-olds (*M* age = 30 months, range = 28–31 months, 15 boys and 13 girls) and twenty-eight 4-year-olds (*M* age = 47 months, range = 46–49 months, 15 boys and 13 girls). Two additional 2½-year-old girls and their mothers were unable to complete one session due to scheduling difficulties and were excluded from the study. Participants were recruited from participant files of infants who had participated in previous studies at Rutgers University and resided within a 60-mile radius of the university. Participants were predominantly middle-class, White families from suburban communities.

Design and Procedure

Each mother–child dyad participated in two sessions within a 2-week period. Four past events were discussed in one session and four future events were discussed in the other session. Order of past and future conversations was counterbalanced.

Two of the four events discussed in each session were designated as *familiar.* These consisted of events experienced at least twice before and included events such as going to the doctor, playing in the snow, visiting a friend, going to birthday parties, and celebrating holidays (for 4-year-olds). The remaining two events discussed during each session were *novel* events. For past conversations, these were events that had been experienced only once and for future conversations, these were events that had either never been experienced or had been experienced only once. Novel events included events such as going to a circus, having chicken pox, going to the farm, and celebrating holidays (2½-year-olds). Depending on individual child's experience, the same event could be either familiar or novel. For example, annual holiday celebrations were often mentioned as novel events for 2½-year-olds, but familiar events for 4-year-olds. For each type of event (past novel, past familiar, future novel, and future familiar), mothers were asked to select events that had occurred or would occur within 2 months from the present so that that the temporal time frame would be similar for all events.

A female experimenter visited participants in their homes for both sessions. At the beginning of each session, the experimenter explained how to select two novel and two familiar events. Mothers were given a sheet of paper to record the event selections (order of novel and familiar events was counterbalanced). Then the experimenter told the mothers, "Just discuss each topic as normally as possible with your child until you feel that the conversation is over." All conversations were tape-recorded. In most cases, the experimenter left the room while the mother and child conversed. Audiotapes were transcribed verbatim for coding.

Coding

Examples of conversations can be seen in the Appendix.

Type of Utterance and Frame of Reference

Each maternal contribution was first coded into one of the following categories (coding scheme adapted by Haden, Haine, & Fivush, 1997 from Reese et al., 1993).

Question.   Any question that requires some kind of input from the child including information questions, yes–no questions, and fill-in-the-blank questions ("Did we go on a train?" "What happens at Grandma's house?").

Contextual statement.   A statement that provides the child with new information about the event ("It was hot that day").

Evaluation.   Confirms or negates a child's previous utterance ("Uh huh").

Prompt.   Provides no content, but prods the child to respond ("What else?").

Memory placeholder.   Statement or question with no memory information ("I don't know").

Metacognitive comment.   Comments on the process of thinking about the past or future ("I forgot that").

Clarification.   Request for clarification from the child ("What did you say?")

Associative talk.   Comments about other events ("I went to a dentist last month").

Unclassifiable.   Utterance does not fall into any other category ("You're not paying attention").

Multiple sentences or clauses were coded separately. For example, if mother said, "That's right, we did see an elephant. What was the elephant doing?" it would coded as an evaluation, repetition, and question.

All questions and contextual statements were coded as to whether they consisted of an elaboration or a repetition. Elaborations referred to new information about the event under discussion; repetitions referred to information previously discussed.

All questions and contextual statements were also coded in terms of the their temporal point of reference using the following criteria.

Past episodes.   Use of the past tense as in "What did you do the last time you went to the playground?"

General event knowledge.   Use of the timeless present tense as in "What happens at preschool?"

Future actions.   Simple use of the future tense, for example, "What are you going to do at the beach?"

Future hypothetical.   Includes references to possible actions ("Maybe we'll see horses there"), predictions ("Do you think Amanda will be there?"), and elicitation of preferences ("Would you like to have a birthday party at McDonald's?")

Temporal Terms

Mother's speech was also coded for five categories of temporal terms.

Episode markers.   References to "last year" or "next time" that served to index which episode of a repeated event was referred to. Although sometimes these included references to conventional time units (e.g., "year"), they did not refer to an interval of time, but simply marked which episode was under discussion.

Conventional time markers.   References to any conventionalized unit of time such as *day, week, month, year, Saturday, July, spring, night,* and *hour.* References to conventional units referring to the immediate 24 hr were coded in a separate category.

Conventional time—within 24 hr.   Because several studies found that immediate temporal references are more common in speech to young children than distant references, references such as *yesterday, today, tomorrow, now, this afternoon, tonight,* and *last night* were coded in a separate category of conventional time references.

Sequence.   Reference to time in terms of a sequence of actions within or between events, such as *after, before, next, then, when we first came in,* and *the last thing.*

Indeterminate interval.   These references referred to an interval of time, but did not code the interval in terms of a conventional time unit, for example, *in a while, soon, after a long while, while I'm gone,* and *a long time ago.*
Temporal references were coded across all utterance categories and the frequency of production was calculated for each event under discussion.

Intercoder Agreement

Two coders independently scored 10 randomly selected transcribed protocols from each age group, including 5 past sessions and 5 future sessions to calculate intercoder agreement. Each session included discussions of four events (two novel and two familiar). In the first wave of coding, each maternal utterance was coded for type of utterance and questions and contextual statements were also coded as elaborations or repetitions and for frame of reference. For this coding, intercoder agreement was 92% for 2½-year-old past sessions, 95% for 2½-year-old future sessions, 94% for 4-year-old past sessions, and 96% for 4-year-old future sessions. In a separate coding, temporal references were identified and coded for type of reference. Intercoder agreement was 91% for 2½-year-old past sessions, 91% for 2½-year-old future sessions, 92% for 4-year-old past sessions, and 94% for 4-year-old future sessions. Differences were discussed and resolved and one investigator, unaware of participants' age and sex, coded the remaining protocols.

RESULTS

The first set of analyses examined variability and consistency in maternal style across past and future conversations. The second set of analyses examined the temporal frames of reference that mothers used across conversations. The final set of analyses tested for differences in mother's use of temporal terms across conversations.

Maternal Style Across Past and Future Conversations

Research on maternal styles in talking about the past has used an elaboration ratio score, which is computed by dividing the number of elaborations produced by the number of repetitions produced (Fivush & Fromhoff, 1988; Hudson, 1990). Separate elaboration scores for past and future conversations were computed for each mother using this formula. A 2 (age of child: 2½ vs. 4) × 2 (conversation: past vs. future) × 2 (interview order: past–future vs. future–past) analysis of variance (ANOVA) produced no significant effects.[1]

Next, to examine consistency in mother's style across conversations, Pearson product–moment correlations between mothers' elaboration scores for past and future conversation were computed for mothers of younger and older children. There was a significant correlation in maternal elaboration over past and future event

---

[1]Event was not included as a variable in this analysis because elaboration ratio scores were not computed separately for novel and familiar events. Instead, the scores were based on total production within each past and future conversations that each included discussions of two novel and two familiar events.

conversations for mothers of 4-year-olds, $r = .41, p < .05$, but not 2½-year-olds, $r = .16, p = .40$. Ratio scores were also used to divide mothers into separate categories of high (HI) or low (LO) elaboration groups by dividing the sample into equal groups of 14 participants for each age group. Means and ranges for each category for each age group are displayed in Table 1. Comparing categorizations across conversations, 32 mothers (16 in each age group) were categorized in the same elaboration group in both conversations, whereas 24 mothers (12 in each age group) were categorized in different groups across conversations. Therefore, there was not a high degree of consistency in maternal elaboration across past and future conversations.

Questions and Contextual Statements: Frequencies and Point of Reference

Questions and contextual statements represent mothers' substantive contributions and are generally considered the most revealing measures of maternal elicitation style (Reese et al., 1993). In general, mothers asked more than three times as many questions ($M = 8.83$) as they provided contextual statements ($M = 2.38$) in each event discussion. Because preliminary analyses indicated that effects were similar across both types of utterance, frequencies were combined in a single, total production measure.

A preliminary 2 (age) × 2 (order) × 2 (maternal style: HI vs. LO) × 2 (conversation) × 2 (event: novel vs. familiar) ANOVA with repeated measures on conversa-

TABLE 1
Means, Standard Deviations, and Ranges of Maternal Elaboration Scores
in Younger and Older, HI and LO Elaboration Groups

Groups	M	SD	Lowest Score	Highest Score
Future conversations				
Mothers of younger children				
LO	3.25	1.14	0.96	4.88
HI	10.39	6.35	5.33	29.00
Mothers of older children				
LO	5.00	1.26	2.41	6.68
HI	13.92	12.81	6.82	49.00
Past conversations				
Mothers of younger children				
LO	2.45	0.66	1.00	3.67
HI	7.49	3.35	4.48	15.00
Mothers of older children				
LO	4.42	1.64	1.08	7.00
HI	11.19	8.15	7.33	42.00

Note. HI = high elaboration group; LO = low elaboration group.

tion and event was performed on the total number of questions and contextual statements. There were no significant main or interaction effects in this analysis. Because total production did not vary significantly across conversations, frequency measures (vs. proportions) were used in all subsequent analyses. Because there were no significant effects for order or for maternal style, these variables were not included in subsequent analyses. To test for differences in temporal frame of reference across conversations, separate 2 (age) × 2 (conversation) × 2 (event) mixed ANOVAs were performed on each of the four temporal frames of reference (past, general, future, and hypothetical), with repeated measures on conversation and event. These data are displayed in Figure 1.

The analysis of use of past reference yielded main effects for conversation, $F(1, 54) = 90.03, p < .001$, and event, $F(1, 54) = 4.41, p < .05$, and a significant Conversation × Event interaction, $F(1, 54) = 12.80, p < .01$. Not surprisingly, past reference was more frequent in past conversations ($M = 38.15, SD = 26.11$) than for future conversations ($M = 5.32, SD = 9.10$). Mothers also referred to the past more often when discussing novel events ($M = 23.65, SD = 18.53$) than familiar events ($M = 19.81, SD = 14.31$). However, Newman–Keuls post hoc tests on the Conversation × Event interaction indicate that event differences were significant only for past conversations, $p < .05$, but not future conversations (see Figure 1).

The analysis of general reference yielded main effects of conversation, $F(1, 54) = 23.56, p < .001$, and event, $F(1, 54) = 19.75, p < .001$, but no significant interaction effects. Mothers used general references more often in future conversations ($M = 17.06, SD = 13.61$) than in past conversations ($M = 8.56, SD = 11.32$), and

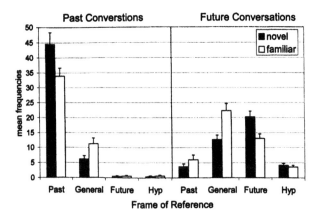

FIGURE 1   Mean frequencies of past, general, future, and hypothetical references in mothers' combined questions and contextual statements for novel and familiar events in past and future conversations (error bars represent the standard errors).

more frequently when discussing familiar events ($M = 16.47$, $SD = 15.42$) than novel events ($M = 9.15$, $SD = 9.55$).

The analysis of future reference produced main effects of conversation, $F(1, 54) = 133.10$, $p < .001$; and event, $F(1, 54) = 17.12$, $p < .001$; and a significant Conversation × Event interaction effect, $F(1, 54) = 17.38$, $p < .001$. As would be expected, mothers referred to the future more often in future conversation ($M = 16.30$, $SD = 12.06$) than in past conversations ($M = 0.55$, $SD = 1.79$). They also referred to the future often when discussing novel events ($M = 10.38$, $SD = 7.38$) than when discussing familiar events ($M = 6.47$, $SD = 6.47$), but Newman–Keuls post hoc tests on the Conversation × Event interaction indicate that the event effect was significant for future conversations ($M = 20.25$, $SD = 13.03$ for novel events and $M = 12.36$, $SD = 11.09$ for familiar events) but not past conversations ($Ms = .50$ and $.59$, $SDs = 1.72$ and 1.85 for novel and familiar events, respectively).

The only significant effect obtained in the analysis of hypothetical reference was a main effect of conversation, $F(1, 54) = 44.72$, $p < .001$. Mothers used hypothetical reference more often in future conversations ($M = 3.71$, $SD = 4.52$) than in past conversations ($M = 0.55$, $SD = 2.13$).

Although it was expected that mothers would refer to the past more in past conversations and to the future more in future conversations, these analyses also show that mothers' use of general and hypothetical reference varied across conversations. Mothers included more general and more hypothetical references when talking about future events than when discussing past events, indicating that temporal reference was more varied in discussions of future events than past events.

Temporal Terms

Frequencies of mention for five categories of temporal terms were analyzed in separate 2 (age) × 2 (conversation) × 2 (event) mixed ANOVAs with repeated measures on conversation and event. These data are displayed in Figure 2.

The analysis of episodic markers yielded a main effect of event, $F(1, 54) = 6.62$, $p < .05$; significant interactions effects of Conversation × Event, $F(1, 54) = 4.38$, $p < .05$; and Conversation × Event × Age, $F(1, 54) = 6.54$, $p < .05$. Separate 2 (conversation) × 2 (event) repeated measures ANOVAs were performed for each age group to further interpret the three-way interaction. There were no significant effects for the younger age group, but the analysis for 4-year-olds yielded a significant main effect of event, $F(1, 27) = 7.08$, $p < .05$, and a significant Conversation × Event interaction effect, $F(1, 27) = 8.05$, $p < .01$. Although mothers of older children used episodic markers more often when discussing future events ($M = 0.80$, $SD = 1.26$) than past events ($M = 0.55$, $SD = 0.92$), Newman–Keuls post hoc tests, $p < .05$, indicate that they used episodic markers significantly more often when discussing future familiar events ($M = 1.36$, $SD = 1.93$) than when discussing both types of past events ($Ms = .57$ and $.54$, $SDs = .84$ and 1.00 for familiar novel events, respectively), but the difference for between past event frequencies was not significant. Frequency of mention for future novel events ($M = 0.25$, $SD = 0.50$) was significantly less than all other groups.

The analysis of conventional temporal terms yielded main effects of conversation, $F(1, 54) = 15.34$, $p < .001$, and age, $F(1, 54) = 6.70$, $p < .05$. Mothers of older children used more conventional terms ($M = 2.21$, $SD = 2.12$) than mothers of younger children ($M = 1.46$, $SD = 1.49$), and there were more conventional terms used in future conversations ($M = 2.46$, $SD = 2.61$) than in past conversations ($M = 1.21$, $SD = 1.52$).

There were no significant effects in the analysis of use of conventional terms consisting of references to the immediate 24 hr.

The analysis of sequence terms produced a main effect of conversation, $F(1, 54) = 6.30$, $p < .05$, but no other significant effects. As shown in Figure 2, sequence terms were used more when talking about the past ($M = 3.76$, $SD = 8.16$) than the future ($M = 1.72$, $SD = 2.63$).

There were no significant effects in the analysis of terms referring to indeterminate intervals.

Therefore, conversation differences were found for conventional time references and sequence terms with greater mention of conventional time markers in

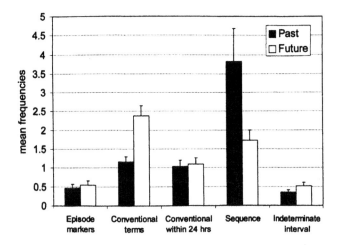

FIGURE 2   Mean frequencies for mention of temporal terms in past and future conversations (error bars represent the standard errors).

discussing future events and greater mention of sequence terms in discussing past events.

DISCUSSION

The temporal language environment that mothers provided for their children across past and future conversations differed in several important ways. Past and future conversations varied with respect to the larger temporal frame of reference within which the events under discussion were placed, different levels of hypothetical talk were mentioned in each type of conversation, and the conversations included different types of temporal language. Therefore, conversations about past and future events provided children with different types of information about how events are situated in time and provided different contexts for learning to conceptualize and talk about time.

With respect to the temporal frame of reference invoked, mother's questions and contextual statements regarding past events were relatively straightforward; the majority of questions and contextual statements were phrased in the past tense, even when discussing familiar events. Mothers rarely used hypothetical references and most of the temporal terms they used consisted of references to event sequence ("before" and "after") and not to conventional references to days, weeks, months, and years. To understand their mothers' questions and to contribute to the discussions, children needed only to understand (a) the difference between the past and the present (i.e., differentiate "then" from "now"); (b) the difference between general event knowledge and memory for a specific episode (i.e., what happens vs. what happened one time); and (c) how sequence terms such as *then, when, before,* and *after* refer to actions within an event sequence. Research has indicated that children generally master these distinctions by the age of 4 years (Hudson & Nelson, 1986; Nelson, 1986, 1993).

In contrast, mothers' temporal language when discussing future events was more complex. Mothers discussed future events, general event knowledge, past memories, and hypothetical events all within a single conversation. When talking about future familiar events, mothers referred to general event knowledge as much as they referred to future actions. Even talk about the past, although less frequent than other temporal references, was included on an average of four times per conversation. Mothers used more hypothetical language to suggest possible actions ("Maybe we'll see Grover there") and elicit predictions ("Who do you think will be there?") and preferences ("Would you like to do that?") in future conversations than in past conversations. Mothers also used conventional terms to denote time (beyond the immediate 24 hr) almost twice as often in discussing future events than when talking about the past.

Therefore, talk about future events was temporally more complex than talk about the past. To follow along, children needed to differentiate specific events in real time from general event knowledge, and understand how events are ordered along a time line that starts before the present and extends into the future with specific points marked along the time line. Children also needed to engage in hypothetical thinking and planning to fully comprehend mothers' talk about the future. The analyses presented here provide no information as to how well children understood mothers' temporal references. Research on children's emerging concepts of conventional time reviewed earlier would suggest that the 2½-year-olds had little understanding of these terms, but that the 4-year-olds were able to make sense of some of these references. Whether or not they fully understood their mothers' temporal references, children were given additional exposure to these concepts when talking about future events, as compared to conversations about the past

On the surface, it is not surprising that mothers used more hypothetical talk in future conversations than in past conversations. However, this finding is important because use of hypothetical reference may indicate mothers' stance toward future events that they communicated to their children. Mothers could simply tell children what is going to happen (and in many cases, they did), but by eliciting children's predictions and preferences, mothers also asked children to think about future events as hypothetical entities including options that have not been determined, but that can be discussed and planned for. Use of hypothetical language may reflect a strategy for engaging children in thinking about the future and for helping children to conceptualize themselves as participants in future events. By discussing what might or could happen and asking children what they thought would happen, or would like to see happen, mothers included their children as active agents in constructing plans for future events. It has been argued that conversations about the past help young children construct a concept of an autobiographic self (Nelson, 1993); conversations about the future may assist children in developing a concept of a future self (Bruner, 1990; Hudson, 2000). Use of hypothetical language may therefore be a marker for a particular style of talking about the future that could affect children's participation in future conversations, have implications for how children learn to plan for future events, and influence children's emerging self-concepts.

As found in previous research, the proportion of elaborations as compared to repetitions in mothers' utterances indicated stylistic differences in how mothers elicited recall from their children. However there was little consistency in maternal elaboration scores across past and future conversations and maternal elaboration ratios did not affect the amount of information mothers provided in either type of conversation. The significance of maternal styles on children's contributions to future conversations awaits further analysis. It is possible that, as in past conversations, a more elaborative maternal style is associated with higher levels of child contributions. It is also possible that an elaborative elicitation style is more important for children's recall of past events, but may not affect children's ability to contribute to discussions about the future. As discussed previously, other maternal speech characteristics such as use of hypothetical reference or reference to general event knowledge may facilitate children's participation in future talk. Additional research on the relation between maternal speech variables and children's contributions will be important for addressing these issues.

The paucity of age effects in these analyses is striking. Although there is considerable evidence that 2- and 4-year-old children vary considerably in their understanding of temporal concepts (Benson, 1997; Friedman, 1977, 1990, 1992), mothers' temporal language was remarkably consistent across both age groups. It would seem reasonable to expect mothers to use less hypothetical talk and fewer temporal references when talking to younger children, but the only significant age effect for these measures was found for mother's use of conventional time terms.

One way to interpret these findings is that mothers may be creating a "zone of proximal development" for their children (Vygotsky, 1978). That is, they are scaffolding discussions in such a way as to include their children's participation and guide children through a discussion of different time frames, using appropriate temporal language, but not necessarily expecting full understanding, as illustrated in the following excerpt from a conversations with a 2½-year-old:

M: In three weeks, Mommy and Daddy are going to go away on a plane and do you know who we are going to see? We are going to see Nicole and Brian and Caroline.

C: Nicole?

M: In England, yeah. But Michael is going to stay home with Oma and Opa. You are going to have a lot of fun. They are going to take you to the parks. They are gonna take you to a movie with popcorn, yeah. And you are gonna visit Grandma and Grandpa for a while when Mommy and Daddy are going to be away for two weeks. *I know you don't know what that means.* And I hope you miss us, but you probably won't, right? [emphasis added]

By using the appropriate temporal language, mothers are providing a learning context for children. These types of conversations may be an important context in which children learn the different ways that language is used to refer to past and future familiar events. Consider how one child is learning the concept of an annual event as mother and child talk about recurring birthday parties in terms of "next time," "next year," and "every year."

M: We're going to talk about your birthday party. What did you do for your birthday party? Do you remember your birthday party? What kind of party did you have? Did you have a Batman party?

C: Yeah.

M: Did you like your party? Yeah? What kind of party do you want next time?

C: I will have another one?

M: Yeah, next year.

C: Next year?

M: Yeah.
C: I want an X-men birthday.
M: An X-men birthday, yeah? Next time? Okay.
C: David will have a birthday coming up.
M: Yeah, David will have a birthday next year. You have a birthday every year.

This example suggests that conversations about upcoming events are a natural context to discuss the cyclical nature of events such as birthdays and holidays and for children to learn how recurring events are referenced in terms of conventional time concepts such as *next year, next summer, next month,* and so on.

Despite the fact that mothers used a variety of temporal frames of reference and temporal terms when talking with both 2½- and 4-year-olds, the finding that they used more conventional temporal terms with older children provides evidence that the zone of proximal development created through use of temporal language was sensitive to children's developmental level. For at least one important aspect of temporal language, the use of conventional and quantifiable temporal terms, mothers provided a more challenging linguistic environment for older children. Further analysis of children's contributions will address the issue of the degree to which mothers' language matches children's temporal understanding.

Although mothers did not vary the temporal frames of reference they used as a function of their children's age, they did talk about novel and familiar events in different ways. This finding also suggests that they were assessing the level of background knowledge children could bring to the conversation and they used different strategies to engage children in future conversations depending on the level of children's knowledge about the events under discussion. By framing the discussion of future events in terms of children's general event knowledge and episodic memories, mothers may be facilitating their children's comprehension and participation (Nelson, 1996).

This study indicates that conversational analysis of parent–child talk about the future is a fruitful approach to understanding how children learn to think about the future. Conversational analyses are particularly informative because we can analyze not only the frequency and variety of temporal references (e.g., tense, aspect, sequence terms, and conventional time terminology) that children hear, but also the ways in which children's participation in thinking about the future is elicited. It is also useful to examine the ways in which future references are juxtaposed to the past and present within a conversation. The degree to which mothers referred to general event knowledge, memories of the past, and predictions for the future within single conversations suggests that they were mentally accessing a temporal representation (i.e., a mental time line) that provided simultaneous reference to the past, present, and future, such as the type of spatial representation proposed by Friedman (1992, 2000). Mothers seemed to assume that children could access a similar representation and that references to past episodes and general event knowledge provided useful background information for children's thinking about the future. Additional analyses of children's participation will provide important data regarding the extent to which children were able to "follow along" by accessing a similar time line representation and can determine whether references to past episodes and general event knowledge facilitated children's participation. The variety of temporal terminology used by mothers when discussing future events also suggests that these conversations provide the type of exposure to conventional temporal language that children need to coordinate experiential time concepts with conventional representations of days of the week, months of the year, seasons, annual events, and historical time (Friedman, 1992; Nelson, 1996). Analysis of children's contributions can help to determine if and how individual differences in mothers' temporal reference affect children's participation in conversations about future events as well as their emerging time concepts.

ACKNOWLEDGMENTS

Portions of this research were presented at the meetings of the Society for Research in Child Development, Washington, D.C., 1997 and Minneapolis, Minnesota, 2001. This research was supported by a faculty research grant from Rutgers University.

I thank Brandi Sosa for her considerable efforts in organizing data collection and coding. I also thank Phyllis Meloro and Margot Burke for their assistance in data collection and coding and Estelle Mayhew who also assisted in coding data. I am especially grateful for the cooperation of the mothers and children who volunteered to participate in this project.

REFERENCES

Bauer, P. J. (1995). Recalling past events: From infancy to early childhood. *Annals of Child Development, 11,* 25–71.

Benson, J. B. (1997). The development of planning: It's about time. In S. L. Friedman & E. K. Scholnick (Eds.), *The developmental psychology of planning: Why, how, and when do we plan?* (pp. 43–75). Mahwah, NJ: Lawrence Erlbaum Associates, Inc.

Benson, J. B., Talmi, A., & Haith, M. M. (1999, April). *Adult speech about events in time: A replication.* Presented at the meetings of the Society for Research in Child Development, Albuquerque, NM.

Bruner, J. (1990). *Acts of meaning.* Cambridge, MA: Harvard University Press.

Engel, S. (1986). *Learning to reminisce: A developmental study of how young children talk about the past.* Unpublished doctoral dissertation, City University of New York Graduate Center, New York.

Farrant, K., & Reese, E. (2000). Maternal style and children's participation in reminiscing: Stepping stones in children's autobiographical memory development. *Journal of Cognition and Development, 1,* 193–225.

Fivush, R. (1997). Event memory in early childhood. In N. Cowan (Ed.), *The development of memory in childhood* (pp. 139–161). Hove East Sussex, England: Psychology Press.

Fivush, R., & Fromhoff, F. (1988). Style and structure in mother–child conversations about the past. *Discourse Processes, 11,* 337–355.

Friedman, W. J. (1977). The development of children's knowledge of cyclic aspects of time. *Child Development, 48,* 1593–1599.

Friedman, W. J. (1986). The development of children's knowledge of temporal structure. *Child Development, 57,* 1386–1400.

Friedman, W. J. (1989). The representation of temporal structure in children, adolescents, and adults. In I. Levin & D. Zakay (Eds.), *Time and human cognition: A life-span perspective. Advances in psychology* (pp. 259–304). Amsterdam: North-Holland.

Friedman, W. J. (1990). Children representations of the pattern of daily activities. *Child Development, 61,* 1399–1412.

Friedman, W. J. (1991). The development of children's memory for the time of past events. *Child Development, 62,* 139–155.

Friedman, W. J. (1992). The development of children's representations of temporal structure. In F. Macar, V. Pouthas, & W. J. Friedman (Eds.), *Time, actions and cognition: Towards bridging the gap* (pp. 67–75). Dordrecht, The Netherlands: Kluwer.

Friedman, W. J. (2000). The development of children's knowledge of the times of future events. *Child Development, 71,* 913–932.

Friedman, W. J., & Brudos, S. L. (1988). On routines and routines: The early development of spatial and temporal representations. *Cognitive Development, 3,* 167–182.

Friedman, W. J., & Kemp, S. (1998). The effects of elapsed time and retrieval on young children's judgments of the temporal distances of past events. *Cognitive Development, 13,* 335–367.

Haden, C. A. (1998). Reminiscing with different children: Relating maternal stylistic consistency and sibling similarity in talk about the past. *Developmental Psychology, 34,* 1366–1371.

Haden, C. A., & Fivush, R. (1996). Contextual variation in maternal conversational styles. *Merrill-Palmer Quarterly, 43,* 200–227.

Haden, C. A., Haine, R. A., & Fivush, R. (1997). Developing narrative structure in parent–child reminiscing across the preschool years. *Developmental Psychology, 33,* 295–307.

Harner, L. (1981). Children talk about time and aspect of actions. *Child Development, 52,* 498–506.

Hudson, J. A. (1990). The emergence of autobiographic memory in mother-child conversation. In R. Fivush & J. A. Hudson (Eds.), *Knowing and remembering in young children* (pp. 166–196). New York: Cambridge University Press.

Hudson, J. A. (1993). Reminiscing with mothers and others: Autobiographical memory in young two-year-olds. *Journal of Narrative and Life History, 3*(1), 1–32.

Hudson, J. A. (2000). The anticipated self: Mother–child talk about future events. In C. Moore & K. Lemmon (Eds.), *The self in time developmental perspectives* (pp. 53–74). Mahwah, NJ: Lawrence Erlbaum Associates, Inc.

Hudson, J., & Nelson, K. (1986). Repeated encounters of a similar kind: Effects of familiarity on children's autobiographic memory. *Cognitive Development, 1,* 253–271.

Lucariello, J., & Nelson, K. (1987). Remembering and planning talk between mothers and children. *Discourse Processes, 10,* 219–235.

MacWhinney, B. (1995). *The CHILDES Project: Tools for analyzing talk.* Mahwah, NJ: Lawrence Erlbaum Associates, Inc.

McCabe, A., & Peterson, C. (1991). Getting the story: A longitudinal study of parental styles in eliciting narratives and developing narrative skill. In A. McCabe & C. Peterson (Eds.), *Developing narrative structure* (pp. 217–253). Hillsdale, NJ: Lawrence Erlbaum Associates, Inc.

Nelson, K. (Ed.). (1986). *Event knowledge: Structure and function in development.* Hillsdale, NJ: Lawrence Erlbaum Associates, Inc.

Nelson, K. (1993). The psychological and social origins of autobiographic memory. *Psychological Science, 4,* 1–8.

Nelson, K. (1996). *Language in cognitive development: The emergence of the mediated mind.* New York: Cambridge University Press.

Reese, E., & Fivush, R. (1993). Parental styles of talking about the past. *Developmental Psychology, 29,* 596–606.

Reese, E., Haden, C. A., & Fivush, R. (1993). Mother-child conversations about the past: Relationships of style and memory over time. *Cognitive Development, 8,* 403–430.

Sachs, J. (1983). Talking about the there and then: The emergence of displaced reference in parent–child discourse. In K. E. Nelson (Ed.), *Children's language* (Vol. 4, pp. 3–28). Hillsdale, NJ: Lawrence Erlbaum Associates, Inc.

Vygotsky, L. S. (1978). *Mind in society: The development of higher psychological processes.* Cambridge, MA: Harvard University Press.

APPENDIX
Examples of Past and Future Conversations

Past Novel Event, 4-Year-Old: Farm Trip

M: Ryan, tell me about Aunt Carrie's farm. What was your job at the farm? Who did you have to feed?

C: Snowdrift.

M: How do you feed Snowdrift?

C: With a bottle.

M: With a bottle, that's right. Mommy makes the bottle with hot water and where does Snowdrift live?

C: In the shed.

M: Does Snowdrift live in the shed? And Ron went down and got Snowdrift out of the shed and then what happened? What happened to Snowdrift in the shed? Did you put her away?

C: No.

M: No, you were trying to teach her how to play hopscotch, weren't you?

C: Yeah.

M: That was pretty funny, huh? How do you teach the lamb to play hopscotch, what did you do?

C: I don't know how to tell you.

M: Tell me.

C: Snips her hair.

M: Who snips her hair?

C: The lambs.

M: The lambs snip their hair? Oh, that's right, Aunt Carrie did give the lambs, she cut their wool.

C: Yeah.

Past Familiar Event, 2½-Year-Old: Bedtime

M: Jamie, I want to ask you something. When you go night-night, does Mommy read a book to you when you go night-night?

C: Yeah.

M: What else? What else do we do? Who's in bed with you when you to sleep?

M: Who sleeps with you?

C: The baby.

M: The baby. Who else sleeps with you? What happened last night while you were sleeping? Jamie, Jamie, what happened last night when you went to bed? How come Mommy had to change all the bed?

C: No.

M: How come?

C: I spit up.

M: You spit up. That's right. Blah! Then what did Mommy do?

C: Mommy cleaned it up.

M: Mommy cleaned it up. Yes I did. Did you feel better then?

C: No.

M: No. So then what did you do? Where did you sleep? Jamie, who did you sleep with last night?

C: I don't know.

M: You don't know. Did you sleep with Mommy?

C: Yeah.

Future Familiar Event, 2½-Year-Old: Going to the Dentist

M: Do you know what we are going to do in the next few months? We are going to visit the dentist.

C: Yeah.

M: You know how Mommy always checks your teeth every night? She helps you brush your teeth? She wants to look inside. She always says, "let the dentist check, open up, honey," right?

C: Yeah.

M: Yeah, that's what I do, and I brush, brush, brush. And last night, who's teeth did we brush?

C: Mommy.

M: Yeah, and who else? Didn't you have all your little friends with you in the bathroom with us?

C: Yeah.

M: Like who? Who's teeth were we brushing besides Michael's teeth?

C: Daddy's

M: No, Daddy wasn't there. Was lion in there?

C: Yes.

M: And all your little friends had their teeth brushed, too, right? And then the dentist looked in and said, "That's a good report, they all have very good teeth." Okay, so one day soon we are doing to go see the dentist. You're gonna sit up in the big chair and he'll say, "Open your mouth wide please" and he's gonna look in.

C: Yeah.

M: And he'll see what kid of condition they are in.

C: Yeah.

M: So we always have to brush our teeth nicely so that when we go to the dentist you have nice shiny teeth to show him.

Future Novel Event, 4-Year-Old: Vacation

M: Maybe in June we're going on vacation. Would you like to do that. Do you want to go on vacation? No ... uhmmm why not, tell me why not?

C: 'Cause I want to stay with my doggies.

M: You do? Well do you remember us going on vacation last year? You and me and Daddy?

C: What about my dog?

M: Well Aunt Sheila took care of the dogs and she can take care of the dogs again. And they'll be, they'll be well taken care of if Aunt Sheila comes and stays her. Will that be okay then? Um, well, do you remember where we went last year on vacation?

C: The mall.

M: The mall, well, we went shopping. But we didn't really go to the mall. Uhmm, we went to the shore. To the beach.

C: I remember that but I got sand toys.

M: Yeah, we got, and we brought lots of sand toys. And what did we do with those toys?

C: We played with them. My dad got sand crabs out of the sand.

M: Right, and do you remember what he did with those?

C: He put them in the water.

M: Oh good well maybe if we go on vacation again, you know, we could find some more, would you like to do that? Would you like to find more crabs?

C: Yes.

M: And what do you have to wear when you go to the beach?

C: Bathing suit.

M: Maybe we'll have to get you a new one. Cause I don't know if the other one fits you.

C: My Minnie one.

M: Yeah, well, we'll have to try it on this year. Will that be okay?

C: Not today.

M: Okay, well no, not today. So we'll um, try that on pretty soon.

JOURNAL OF COGNITION AND DEVELOPMENT, 3(1), 73–90

Remembering to Relate: Socioemotional Correlates of Mother–Child Reminiscing

Robyn Fivush and Anjali Vasudeva
Department of Psychology
Emory University

Previous research has established that mothers vary in how elaborately they reminisce with their preschool children, but explanation of these individual differences is lacking. We predicted that maternal elaborations during reminiscing would be related to mother–child attachment status, as well as to measures of verbal and nonverbal emotional expressiveness. Thirty-eight middle class mothers and their 4½-year-old children participated in a reminiscing task and a joint art activity, and mothers completed the *Attachment Behavior Q-set* (Waters, 1987). Mothers who were more elaborative during reminiscing also reported a more secure attachment bond, but these variables were unrelated to either verbal or nonverbal expression of emotion during mother–child interaction. However, patterns of relations also varied by gender of child. Theoretical implications of these results for understanding joint reminiscing and attachment are discussed.

Just two decades ago, a revolution occurred in our understanding of children's memory. Against a backdrop of Piagetian and information processing approaches to the development of deliberate memory, Katherine Nelson (1986; Nelson & Gruendel, 1981) argued for a functional approach, focusing on how children use memory in everyday interactions to guide behavior. Rather than examining memory for often meaningless material, Nelson argued that memory was used in the service of self-generated motivated behavior to accomplish both cognitive and social goals. A wealth of theoretical and empirical work on memory development has stemmed from this fundamental paradigm shift. We now know that toddlers and preschoolers have organized, generalized memories of routine and recurring events (e.g., Bauer, 1997; Fivush, 1997; Hudson, 1986; Nelson, 1986), as well as detailed memories of specific, one-time occurrences

---

Requests for reprints should be sent to Robyn Fivush, Department of Psychology, Emory University, Atlanta, GA 30322. E-mail: psyrf@emory.edu

(e.g., Fivush, 1993; Hudson, 1986; Nelson & Ross, 1980; Peterson & Bell, 1996).

Along with a new understanding of memory, this work also focused researchers on the social and cultural contexts in which memory developed (Nelson, 1993, 1996). If children are using memory to accomplish goals in ongoing interactions, then it follows that we must look to these interactions as sites within which memory develops. Indeed, recent research has abundantly demonstrated that children are learning the forms and functions of memory through participating in adult-guided interactions (Nelson & Fivush, 2000). More specifically, children are learning to narrate their past experiences through participating in joint reminiscing with their parents. The ways in which parents structure conversations about past events with their preschool children has been shown to have a profound effect on the ways in which children come to remember their past and share it with others (Engel, 1986; Fivush, 1991; Fivush & Fromhoff, 1988; Hudson, 1990; McCabe & Peterson, 1991; Reese, Haden, & Fivush, 1993). Mothers who have a highly elaborative style, providing rich descriptive detail about past events, provide children with an embellished framework for co-constructing their past, and, with development, these children come to tell richly detailed stories of their own lives. In contrast, mothers who have a less-elaborate reminiscing style, repeating the same questions and providing little embellishment, have children who come to report their past in a more sparse manner. Although much of this work has focused on the mnemonic consequences of maternal reminiscing style, less is understood about the origins of these maternal differences. Why are some mothers more elaborative when reminiscing about the past with their young children than other mothers?

In considering the function of reminiscing about our shared experiences, it seems that memory, in and of itself, may not be the major goal. Rather we choose to reminisce with others to create and maintain social and emotional bonds (e.g., Fivush, 1988; Fivush, Haden, & Reese, 1996; Nelson, 1993, 1996). Through constructing and reconstructing our past with others, we intertwine our experiences, memories, and lives. If this interpretation is correct, then we would predict relations between maternal reminiscing style and other aspects of the mother–child socioemotional relationship. In particular, we would predict that there would be a relation between reminiscing and attachment.

Attachment is clearly a foundational construct in developmental psychology. Decades of research have established both the ontogenesis and the consequences of the mother–child attachment bond (see Cassidy & Shaver, 1999, for an overview). Mothers who are appropriately sensitive to their children's needs and respond contingently, both temporally and affectively, develop a secure attachment bond with their infants. In turn, securely attached infants are able to venture out into the physical and emotional world more comfortably and competently. In contrast, mothers who are less sensitive and appropriate in their responding engender a less-secure attachment relationship, and their children are more anxious and avoidant when faced with new challenges. Again, the underlying assumption is that a secure attachment provides children with a predictable and secure base from which to explore whatever developmental hurdles may arise (Ainsworth, Blehar, Waters, & Wall, 1978).

More recent theoretical approaches to the developing mother–child attachment bond has stressed the importance of mother–child communication (e.g., Bowlby, 1988; Bretherton, 1990, 1999; Thompson, 2000). Whereas the early attachment bond is assumed to be nonconscious, based on sensorimotor associations, with development these interactions become internalized as working models, or narratives of relationships. Securely attached dyads are assumed to be better able to engage in open communication and to integrate negative experiences with more positive ones (Bretherton, 1990; Main, Kaplan, & Cassidy, 1985; see Pillemer, 1998, for a review). More specifically, theorists have argued that parent–child co-constructed narratives provide much of the basis for children's subsequent attachment narratives (e.g., Bretherton, 1990; Thompson, 2000). Related to this, in response to a story stem or probe about parent–child relationships, children who are securely attached narrate more complete, consistent, and coherent narratives, especially about emotionally difficult material (Main, 1991; Waters, Rodriguez, & Ridgeway, 1998), and this difference persists into adulthood (Main, Kaplan, & Cassidy, 1985). Yet little research has examined the content or organization of parent–child co-constructed narratives from an attachment perspective. Koren-Karie, Oppenheim, Haimovich, and Etzion-Carasso (in press) developed a coding scheme for examining the emotional match or mismatch between parents and children in co-constructing stories about emotional experiences. They found that dyads who were securely attached early in development were better able to co-construct coherent, emotionally attuned accounts of past experiences during middle childhood than insecurely attached dyads, suggesting a link between attachment status and quality of parent–child communication.

In addition to emotional attunement, attachment theorists might also predict that securely attached dyads would display more elaborated reminiscing. A secure attachment bond might provide the basis for parents and children to engage in embellished and detailed communication about the past. Similarly, memory theorists would predict that a more elaborated reminiscing style would lead to children's developing ability to represent their past experiences and their past relationships in more detailed and predictable ways, thereby creating and maintaining coherent attachment narratives. Therefore, from multiple theoretical perspectives, there is reason to believe that a more elaborated reminiscing style is related to a more secure attachment bond.

Indeed, one study has now established such a link. Farrant and Reese (2000) examined attachment status at age 18 months and maternal reminiscing style at 18 months, 2 years, 2½ years, and 3½ years. Overall, mothers from more securely attached dyads showed more elaborated reminiscing at all ages. Most interesting, whereas securely attached dyads showed increasing bidirectional relations between mother and child in reminiscing style over time, dyads with insecure attachments showed few bidirectional relations, suggesting that these mothers and children were not as "in tune" and therefore were not able to reciprocally influence each other's reminiscing. These findings also pointed to the necessity of examining both mothers and children, as both reminiscing and attachment must be considered an aspect of the dyad and not just of the mother or the child alone. Therefore a major objective of this study is to examine empirically the relation between maternal elaborativeness, children's participation in reminiscing, and attachment status in preschool children.

There is also reason to predict relations between attachment status and the emotional content of reminiscing. Previous research has established individual differences in the extent to which parents include emotional aspects of the past when reminiscing with their young children (Adams, Kuebli, Boyle, & Fivush, 1995; Fivush, Brotman, Buckner, & Goodman, 2000) and, importantly, parents who talk more about emotions early in development, have children who talk more about emotions later in development (Dunn, Brown, & Beardsall, 1991; Kuebli, Butler, & Fivush, 1995).

From an attachment perspective, it may not be emotion talk, per se, that is critical, but the ability to integrate both positive and negative emotions coherently. Based on both theoretical and empirical work, we would expect more securely attached dyads to be able to discuss emotions more openly, and this may be especially true for negative emotions. As Pillemer (1998) argued, within securely attached dyads, negative emotions can be discussed and resolved because they would be less threatening than for less securely attached dyads. In contrast to this prediction, however, Farrar, Fasig, and Welch-Ross (1997) found that mother–daughter dyads who were insecurely attached discussed more negative events than securely attached mother–daughter dyads. Securely attached mother–daughter dyads discussed both negative and positive events in equal depth. Importantly, there were no relations between attachment status and emotion talk for mother–son dyads, suggesting that gender may be a critical filter through which attachment and reminiscing style must be viewed. More recently, Laible and Thompson (2000) found that more securely attached dyads incorporated more talk about emotion into discussions of the child's past transgressions. They argued that a secure attachment provides the base for communicating about emotionally difficult and threatening material. Therefore a second objective of this study was to further examine how emotion talk might be related to attachment and to reminiscing.

Moreover, if maternal reminiscing style is reflective of the emotional relationship between the mother and child, then we may also expect to see relations to nonverbal aspects of emotional communication. More specifically, mother–child dyads who are more elaborate in reminiscing may also show more positive emotionality or warmth in their nonverbal behavior during joint interactions. Similarly, warmth of interaction may be reflective of the underlying attachment bond. There is actually some theoretical controversy over this relation. In Ainsworth et al.'s (1978) original formulation of the attachment construct, timing of maternal responsiveness was the critical variable, but subsequent theorists have included the emotional tone of the response as well (see Soloman & George, 1999, for a discussion). In examining the emotional attunement of parent–child conversations, Koren-Karie et al. (in press) pointed out that some dyads who displayed high emotional attunement did not seem to display much warmth in their relationship. Therefore, the empirical relations between attachment, warmth, and emotional communication remain open. In this study, we assessed both mothers' and children's nonverbal expressions of warmth toward each other. Although we assumed that higher warmth might be related to both more secure attachment and more elaborated reminiscing, this was really an exploratory aspect of the study.

Finally, we examined relations among attachment, elaborative reminiscing, emotion talk, and warmth as a function of gender. Although gender has not been found to play a major role in mother–child attachment patterns, gender has been critical in understanding maternal reminiscing. Several studies have demonstrated that parents are more elaborate and more emotional when reminiscing with daughters than with sons (Fivush et al., 2000; Reese, Haden, & Fivush, 1996). Furthermore, as discussed earlier, Farrar et al. (1997) found different patterns of relations between emotion talk and attachment in mother–daughter and mother–son dyads. Therefore, it was of interest to examine whether patterns of relations among these variables might differ as a function of the gender of the child.

In summary, there is good theoretical reason to believe that maternal reminiscing style will be related to attachment status such that more securely attached dyads will engage in more elaborated reminiscing. It also seems likely that more securely attached dyads will be better able to integrate positive and negative emotion in their reminiscing about the past, and possibly that nonverbal expression of warmth will also be related to reminiscing, attachment, and emotional integration. Finally, because previous research has established that gender may influence these relations, we examined relations among these constructs for males and females separately.

METHOD

Participants

The data for this study were a subset of data collected for a larger project examining mother–child communications about ongoing and past events. In the larger study, 58 mostly White middle class families with a 4-year-old child (*M* age = 4 years 1 month) participated in one home visit and two laboratory visits during which various parent–child interactions were elicited and observed. We chose to examine 4-year-old children because, by this age, children are quite competent at participating in reminiscing conversations and therefore we could easily assess children's role in these interactions. For the purposes of this study, we examined three aspects of the larger data set, described in more detail later: an elicited mother–child conversation about past events, a videotaped interaction of mother and child engaging in a joint art activity, and the mothers' responses to the *Attachment Behavior Q-set* (Waters, 1987). Nine mothers did not complete all tasks relevant to this analysis. Furthermore, because the videotape was coded for maternal and child nonverbal expression of warmth (as described later) only those taped interactions in which the mother's and child's faces were visible to the camera could be included in this analysis. Based on this criterion, an additional 12 mother–child dyads were eliminated from inclusion in this study, yielding 37 mother–child dyads, 19 girls and 18 boys. All families gave fully informed consent and received a small gift for participating.

Procedure

Mother–child reminiscing.   All families were first visited in their homes and during this visit, the mother was asked to sit in a quiet place with her child and to discuss two specific events that they had experienced together in the past. Mothers were encouraged to select events that were distinctive and that spanned no longer than 1 day, and they were asked to discuss these events in as natural a way as possible for as long as they wished. As in previous research on maternal reminiscing style, no further instructions were given and no further restrictions were placed on the types of events mothers selected (e.g., Fivush & Fromhoff, 1988; Reese et al., 1993). In this way, we were able to obtain the least restrictive view on how mothers and children might reminisce in more everyday naturalistic contexts. However, this also limited the types of events discussed. The vast majority of events discussed (well over 90%) were highly positive, child-centered events such as family outings to visit special friends or relatives; trips to museums, zoos, aquariums; and so forth. Most conversations were approximately 15-min long, and were audiotaped and transcribed verbatim.

Mother–child joint activity.   About 2 weeks after the initial home visit, mothers and children visited a laboratory playroom, where they engaged in a highly interactive "wizard" activity. Mothers and children followed a series of clues that led to activities such as dress up and face painting, building a castle and creating an art collage. The entire event took approximately 40 min and was videotaped. For this study, the art collage activity was coded. This activity involved the mother and child sitting at a child-sized table and creating a collage using markers, sparkles, glue, and stickers. Mothers and children were provided with the materials and were free to construct the collage in any way they chose. The activity took approximately 10 min.

We selected this activity for several reasons. We wanted to obtain a measure of maternal and child nonverbal warmth during an interaction in which they were jointly focused on a common activity. Because our major measure of warmth was glances (as described in detail in the coding section), it did not make sense to examine warmth during reminiscing during which the mother and child spend most of their time looking at each other. Rather, we needed to select an activity during which the mother and child were focused on a common set of objects but would, at least occasionally, look up at each other and communicate nonverbally about their involvement with each other and the activity. Furthermore, for pragmatic purposes we needed to select an activity during which both the mother's and child's face would be visible to the camera for a reasonably extended period of time for coding purposes. Because the art activity involved sitting at a table, this activity was ideal.

Attachment Behavior Q-set.   At the end of the first laboratory visit, mothers were asked to return in 2 weeks and told that at the next visit, they would be asked to rate their children's behaviors on a number of dimensions. They were then given a list of the 90 child behavior descriptions that comprise the *Attachment Behavior Q-set* (Waters, 1987) and asked to read them over and to pay attention to these behaviors over the next couple of weeks. When mothers returned to the laboratory 2 weeks later, they were asked to sort these 90 specific behaviors on a 9-point scale ranging from 1 (*does not describe my child at all*) to 9 (*describes my child very well*), with 10 items in each category. These responses were scored according to standardized criteria yielding a score from 0 to 1, with 1 representing a secure attachment. Note that although this measure was originally designed to be completed by a trained observer, Teti and McGourty (1996) showed that mothers are a reliable source for attachment information, and previous research has used mothers as primary observers (Farrar et al., 1997; Laible & Thompson, 2000).

Coding

Two aspects of mother–child reminiscing were of interest for this study: elaboration and emotional integration.

Elaboration.   All maternal and child utterances were divided into propositional units, defined as subject–verb constructions, and each proposition was coded for content. Based on previous research, two kinds of maternal utterances are critical in determining maternal reminiscing style: elaborations and repetitions (Fivush & Fromhoff, 1988; Reese et al., 1993). Elaborations express how much new information mothers are bringing into the conversations, and how richly detailed the conversations are, whereas repetitions capture the extent to which mothers are simply asking the same questions over and over. As discussed previously, we assumed that more elaborated discussions by both mother and child would be related to more secure attachment. In line with previous research, an elaboration was defined as the provision of any new information. For example, the mother asks, "What did we see at the aquarium?" and then asks, "Did we see those little penguins?" and again, "Those little black and white penguins?" A repetition, in contrast, was simply asking the same question again, as in "What did we see at the aquarium?" and then "What did we see there?" Similarly, the extent to which children provided new memory information was also of interest, and therefore all child utterances that expressed new information were coded as elaborations (e.g., the mother asks "What did we see at the aquarium?" and the child responds "Whales."). Child utterances that repeated what either the mother or child had previously recalled were coded as repetitions (e.g., mother asks "Did we see zebras at the zoo?" and the child responds, "Zebras.").

Ten of the 38 transcripts were coded by two independent raters who achieved 88% agreement (range = 77%–94%). The remaining transcripts were coded by a single rater. Because the overall number of maternal elaborations and repetitions were correlated with each other, $r = .60, p < .01$, and with total number of propositions overall ($r = .98$ for elaborations and .83 for repetitions, both p's $< .01$), overall level of maternal elaboration was conceptualized as the ratio of elaborations to repetitions, calculated as number of elaborations divided by the sum of the number of elaborations and the number of repetitions, similar to previous research (Reese et al., 1993). This ratio measure captures the extent that mothers are elaborating rather then repeating their previous utterances. As also in previous research for children, the frequency of elaborations was assessed to capture the extent to which children were participating in these conversations by providing details about their past experiences, and frequency of repetitions assessed the extent to which children were simply engaged in talking during reminiscing but not providing any new information. It should be noted that number of repetitions was perfectly correlated with number of overall propositions, $r = 1.00$, so repetitions also provided a measure of overall talkativeness.

Emotional integration.   The second dimension of these conversations that was of interest was emotional integration. All mention of emotion words by both mother and child was counted as expressing either positive emotion (happy, fun, love) or negative emotion (sad, angry, scared, etc.). Two coders counted words in 10 of the 38 transcripts and achieved 96% agreement (range = 90%–100%). Number of positive emotion words and negative emotion words used were correlated, $r = .57, p < .05$, and both number of positive emotion words and number of negative emotion words were highly correlated with total number of emotion words used, $r = .97, p < .001$ for positive words to total and, $r = .76, p < .001$ for negative words to total. Because attachment theory predicts that securely attached dyads will be better able to engage in emotionally open conversations, we were especially interested in how positive and negative emotions would be integrated in these conversations. Therefore, we calculated the percentage of positive emotions over all emotion words used to capture the extent to which positive and negative emotion talk was balanced in these conversations. As we predicted that securely attached dyads would be better able to discuss negative as well as positive emotions, we expected they would display a lower percentage of positive emotion words overall than less securely attached dyads. Unfortunately, children used so few emotion words overall in these conversations ($M < 1.0$ per child) that we were only able to examine maternal expression of emotion.

Nonverbal expression of warmth.   We examined mother's nonverbal expressions of positive emotionality, or warmth during the joint art activity with her child. We adapted a coding scheme from Carton and Carton (1998) that captures the extent to which mothers express positive engagement with their child, and includes the following categories:

1. Glances, which are the number of times that the mother looks at her child's face when not speaking together. This category assesses the extent to which the mother "checks in" with her child during a joint activity to assess her child's state.
2. Positive facial expressions, which include smiles and laughs, wide eyes, open mouth, and open, anticipatory expressions.

We also coded for negative expressions, frowns, and so on, but these were virtually nonexistent due to the nature of the activity. Children's nonverbal interactions with their mothers were coded into the same categories. Two raters independently coded 10 mothers and 10 children (from different dyads) and achieved 87.6% agreement on mothers (range = 80%–93%) and 95% agreement on children (range = 92%–100%). Because glances and positive facial expressions were highly intercorrelated, $r = .72, p < .001$, for mothers and, $r = .56, p < .01$, for children, the categories were totaled into one variable expressing maternal warmth. Moreover, although most dyads engaged in the art activity for a minimum of 10 min, a few did not, and therefore, the total number of maternal and child warmth indicators were divided by the number of minutes of engagement in the art activity.

Therefore, overall we quantified three variables for the mother: From the reminiscing conversation we calculated level of elaboration and number of emotion words and, from the joint art activity we calculated maternal nonverbal warmth. Three variables were quantified for the child: From the reminiscing conversation we calculated number of elaborations and number of repetitions, and from the joint art activity, we calculated child nonverbal warmth. In addition, we calculated one dyadic measure: the attachment score.

RESULTS

The analyses addressed two major questions. First, what are the relations between maternal reminiscing style and socioemotional aspects of the mother–child relationship, and, second, how are mothers and children's reminiscing and socioemotional styles related? In addition, we were interested in whether these relations might differ by gender of child. Before presenting the correlational analyses, we present means and standard deviations for all variables in Table 1. In addition to the emotional integration ratio, we also present the mean number of positive and negative emotions words for descriptive purposes.

As can be seen, this was a highly elaborative group of mothers who scored in the midrange of attachment. It is not clear why this group of mothers were so highly elaborative; certainly they are much higher than comparable samples using the same coding scheme. However, as demonstrated in the following, even with this restricted range, we still found significant relations to some of the other variables. Children were also highly elaborative in this sample, as evidenced by the relatively low number of repetitions used during reminiscing. This suggests that mothers and children were highly engaged in the joint reminiscing task.

Maternal use of emotion words was generally low, and mothers were generally balanced in their use of positive and negative emotion words. Finally, as a group,

TABLE 1
Means and Standard Deviations for Maternal
and Child Variables by Gender

	Boys[a]		Girls[b]		Total[c]	
Variable	M	SD	M	SD	M	SD
Attachment	0.43	0.14	0.38	0.16	0.40	0.15
Maternal						
Elaboration ratio	0.91	0.04	0.91	0.05	0.91	0.06
Positive emotion words	2.50	2.82	2.36	2.21	2.43	2.50
Negative emotion words	0.78	0.91	0.76	1.05	0.77	0.98
Emotional integration	0.53	0.38	0.57	0.38	0.55	0.38
Warmth	3.90	1.60	4.10	3.20	3.99	2.54
Child						
Elaborations	18.25	9.50	17.08	9.99	17.65	9.65
Repetitions	2.33	2.18	2.16	1.94	2.24	2.03
Warmth	1.38	0.78	1.31	1.07	1.34	0.92

[a]$n = 18$. [b]$n = 19$. [c]$n = 37$.

TABLE 2
Correlations Among Maternal Variables by Gender

Sample	Attachment	Elaboration	Emotional Integration	Warmth
Total sample				
Attachment	1.00			
Elaboration	0.39***	1.00		
Emotional integration	0.02	–0.19	1.00	
Warmth	0.14	0.19	0.02	1.00
With boys				
Attachment	1.00			
Elaboration	0.39*	1.00		
Emotional integration	0.24	–0.37	1.00	
Warmth	0.45**	–0.17	0.49**	1.00
With girls				
Attachment	1.00			
Elaboration	0.38***	1.00		
Emotional integration	–0.15	–0.06	1.00	
Warmth	0.03	0.32	–0.20	1.00

$*p < .10.$ $**p < .05.$ $***p < .01.$

these mothers appeared to exhibit high levels of nonverbal warmth, smiling and looking at their children about once every 15 sec. Children did not exhibit as much warmth as mothers, smiling and glancing at their mothers once per 1 min, indicating that children were more engaged in the art activity than with their mothers. There were no significant differences in maternal variables with girls versus boys, and nor were there any gender differences between the children as determined by a series of t tests.

Maternal Variables

Table 2 presents correlations among the maternal variables for the sample as a whole and by gender. As can be seen, there is a significant positive correlation between maternal level of elaboration and attachment status, such that mothers who report more secure attachment relations also exhibit more elaborated reminiscing. However, no other correlations approach significance.[1]

As discussed previously, there is reason to believe that the gender of the child may play a role in how these variables are related. Therefore we computed correla-

---

[1]Although from a theoretical perspective, we argue that emotional integration is the appropriate measure of emotion talk in these conversations, we also examined relations with number of positive and number of negative emotion words used in these conversations. No significant correlations between the number of positive, negative, or total number of emotion words and attachment, maternal elaboration, or warmth were obtained.

tions among these variables for boys and girls separately, as displayed in the bottom panels of Table 2. For both boys and girls, maternal level of elaboration is still related to attachment status, although both of these correlations now only approach conventional levels of significance due to decreased power. For girls, there are still no other significant correlations among the variables. For boys, however, attachment status is also significantly related to maternal warmth, as is emotional integration. Mothers who display more nonverbal expressions of warmth during a joint activity with their sons also report more secure attachment relationships and use a higher percentage of positive emotion words when reminiscing than mothers who display less warmth. Yet there is also some suggestion that mothers of sons who are more elaborative during reminiscing use a lower proportion of positive emotion words as well, $r = -.37, p = .12$.

Child Variables

Children's warmth is marginally related to attachment, $r = .30, p = .08$, and this pattern holds for boys and girls. Children's elaborations and repetitions are also correlated, $r = .37, p < .05$. However, when examined by gender, the correlation between child elaborations and repetitions remains significant for boys, $r = .55, p < .05$, but not for girls, $r = .18, p = .47$. These differences suggest that for boys, amount of new information provided during reminiscing is related to overall talkativeness, but this does not seem to be the case for girls. For boys, warmth is also positively related to child repetitions, $r = .42, p < .05$. Finally, for girls, child repetitions are negatively correlated with attachment, $r = -.55, p < .05$, indicating that girls from more securely attached dyads use fewer repetitions during reminiscing.

Relations Between Mothers and Children

Table 3 displays the correlations between maternal and child variables. More elaborative mothers have children who use fewer repetitions and mothers who use a higher proportion of positive emotion terms have children who provide more memory elaborations. However, as can also be seen in Table 3, when examined by gender, these relations only hold for mother–daughter dyads. There are no relations between maternal reminiscing style and child variables in mother–son dyads, but there is a tendency for maternal and child warmth to be positively related. Furthermore, mothers of girls who use a higher proportion of positive emotion during reminiscing show less warmth during a joint activity.

DISCUSSION

The major purpose of this research was to begin to understand why some mothers are more highly elaborative when reminiscing with their young children than other

TABLE 3
Correlations Between Maternal and Child Variables by Gender

| | Maternal Variables | | |
Child Variables	Elaboration Ratio	Emotional Integration	Warmth
Total sample			
Elaboration	0.01	0.41***	0.07
Repetition	−.34*	0.16	−0.01
Warmth	0.02	0.23	0.21
With boys			
Elaboration	0.05	0.19	0.21
Repetition	−0.17	0.05	0.06
Warmth	−0.09	0.05	0.38*
With girls			
Elaboration	−0.04	0.61***	0.01
Repetition	−0.49**	0.29	−0.05
Warmth	0.15	−0.64***	0.12

*$p < .10$. **$p < .05$. ***$p < .01$.

mothers. The results support the idea that maternal reminiscing style is, at least partly, a function of the mother–child emotional relationship. More highly elaborative mothers also reported a more secure attachment bond with their preschool child than did less elaborative mothers, and this pattern held for both boys and girls. Therefore, similar to Farrant and Reese (2000), this study confirms that attachment and reminiscing are related. Of course, these results do not allow us to determine whether more securely attached dyads allow for more elaborated communication, or if more elaborate communication helps create a more secure attachment bond. Farrant and Reese's (2000) longitudinal analysis suggested that it is a secure attachment that allows for more elaborated reminiscing, at least early in development. Further longitudinal research is necessary to elucidate these developing relations.

Surprisingly, we found no relations between emotion talk during reminiscing and attachment status. We had assumed that more securely attached dyads would be able to communicate in more open ways, and especially that they would be better able to incorporate negative emotion in their conversations. Previous research had demonstrated relations between the emotional valence of events discussed and attachment status in mother–daughter dyads but not in mother–son dyads (Farrar et al., 1997). Of course, it must be pointed out that, because of the nature of the task used in this study, conversations focused on highly positive events. It would be intriguing in future research to examine more negative or stressful events. Laible and Thompson (2000) found that securely attached dyads discussed more emotional content in conversations about children's transgressions, supporting the idea that emotionally difficult material might highlight attachment issues. It may be in situations in which mothers and children are discussing highly stressful or traumatic events that differences in the ability to regulate negative emotion may arise and vary as a function of attachment status (e.g., Bowlby, 1988). In addition, we did not find an overall relation between maternal nonverbal positive emotionality, or warmth and attachment status, but children who displayed more warmth during a joint activity tended to be more securely attached. Thus, there is some suggestion that a more secure attachment may be related to more positive nonverbal affect in children.

These overall patterns must be interpreted within light of several gendered patterns obtained. Mothers of sons who had a more secure attachment did display more nonverbal warmth than less securely attached mother–son dyads, but there was no relation for mother–daughter dyads. Intriguingly, mothers of sons who displayed more nonverbal positive affect also talked about a higher proportion of positive emotions during reminiscing. Therefore with sons, mothers seem to display an integrated affective style, with both verbal and nonverbal expressions of positive affect related. Yet, mothers of sons who were more elaborative during reminiscing also tended to use a higher proportion of negative emotion words than less elaborative mothers, suggesting a greater ability to balance positive and negative aspects of past events when reminiscing. This pattern suggests that emotional expression may function differently in different contexts, especially between mothers and sons. Although overall levels of attachment security do not vary by gender, it may very well be that the ways in which attachment and reminiscing style are expressed and related to other variables differ by gender.

Surprisingly, there were no relations between maternal reminiscing style and boys' participation in reminiscing. Moreover, although child elaborations and repetitions were correlated for boys, they were not correlated for girls. For boys, then, there seems to be an underlying dimension of talkativeness, but for girls, memory elaborations and memory repetitions seem to serve different functions. Girls' memory elaborations are related to mothers' focus on positive as compared to negative emotion. Therefore for mothers and daughters, conversations more focused on positive emotionality were related to daughters discussing the event in more detailed and embellished ways. Yet girls who used more memory repetitions were from less securely attached dyads. This suggests that, for girls, memory repetitions may not express an overall level of involvement in reminiscing, but instead represent less emotional engagement in reminiscing.

Previous research has demonstrated that mothers tend to be more elaborative when reminiscing with daughters than with sons, and girls tend to recall more about past events that do boys (Fivush, 1998; Reese et al., 1996). In this study, we found no overall gender differences, either in the ways that mothers interacted with daughters versus sons, or between the girls and boys themselves. Still, the different patterns of relations between mother–son and mother–daughter dyads suggests that there may be different processes or pathways by which dyads come to engage in reminiscing, and these may be somewhat gendered. Harley and Reese (1999) recently argued for individual pathways into autobiographical memory based on longitudinal patterns that suggest that reminiscing emerges from different origins in different children. Although they did not discover gendered patterns, our results support their interpretation of individual pathways. In particular, the ways in which mothers integrate emotions into reminiscing may have differential effects on children's participation. Whether gender proves to be a critical variable in these developing individual differences is an empirical question, but what is clear is that parent–child reminiscing is a complex behavior that emerges from, and contributes to, a large variety of other developmental processes and achievements.

Regardless of the within-gender patterns, the major finding in this study is the relation between maternal level of elaboration during reminiscing and attachment. Several attachment theorists have begun to argue for a narrative perspective to attachment (Bretherton & Mulholland, 1999; Thompson, 2000), and several memory researchers have argued that reminiscing is a social activity that creates and maintains emotional bonds (Fivush, 1994; Fivush et al., 1996; Nelson, 1993, 1996; Pillemer, 1998). The results of this study confirm that this is an appropriate theoretical approach. Moreover, these results point to a possible mechanism by which attachment and narrative are related. As previous research has amply demonstrated, children of highly elaborative mothers come to tell their own life stories in richly detailed and coherent narrative forms (Fivush, 1991; Harley & Reese, 1999; Reese et al., 1993). Because securely attached children are more likely to engage in elaborated parent-guided reminiscing, they are more likely to learn the skills necessary for telling more elaborated and coherent narratives about their own past. Moreover, it may not only be the skills that children are learning in these conversations, but also the value of reminiscing. Children of highly elaborative mothers may be learning that reminiscing is an important and integral part of social interactions, and that it is desirable and enjoyable to share your past experiences with others (see Fivush et al., 1996, for further discussion of this point). Therefore, it is not surprising that more securely attached children tell more coherent and elaborate narratives of their past.

Of course we must be cautious in generalizing these results beyond Western, middle class families. There is accumulating evidence that both attachment (van Ijzendoorn & Sagi, 1999) and maternal reminiscing style (Han, Leichtman, & Wang, 1998; Mullen & Yi, 1995) differs by culture, and clearly the relations between these variables are likely to differ as well. The important point here, however, is that this is a fruitful area of inquiry. Narratives may provide a way of exploring both the bases and the consequences of attachment in culturally sensitive ways.

Perhaps most important, in accord with Katherine Nelson's (1993, 1996) theoretical perspective, this research demonstrates that remembering occurs within a socioemotional and cultural context. In reminiscing with those we share the past with, we intertwine our present lives with our past, and ourselves with others.

Mothers and children who are securely attached and engage in elaborated reminiscing create bonds based on rich stories of shared lives.

ACKNOWLEDGMENT

We are grateful to Sharon Bhandari, Trina Brown, and Janine Buckner for help in collecting, transcribing, and coding data.

REFERENCES

Adams, S., Kuebli, J., Boyle, P., & Fivush, R. (1995). Gender differences in parent–child conversations about past emotions: A longitudinal investigation. *Sex Roles, 33,* 309–323.

Ainsworth, M. D. S., Blehar, M., Waters, E., & Wall, S. (1978). *Patterns of attachment: A psychological study of the strange situation.* Hillsdale, NJ: Lawrence Erlbaum Associates, Inc.

Bauer, P. (1997). Development of memory in early childhood. In N. Cowan (Ed.), *The development of memory in childhood* (pp. 83–112). Sussex, England: Psychology Press.

Bowlby, J. (1988). *A secure base: Clinical applications of attachment theory.* London: Routledge.

Bretherton, I. (1990). Open communication and internal working models: Their role in the development of attachment relationships. In R. A. Thompson (Ed.), *Nebraska Symposium on Motivation: Vol. 36. Socioemotional development* (pp. 59–113). Lincoln: University of Nebraska Press.

Bretherton, I. (1993). From dialogue to representation: The intergenerational construction of self in relationships. In C. A. Nelson (Ed.), *Minnesota Symposium on Child Psychology: Vol. 26. Memory and affect in development* (pp. 237–263). Hillsdale, NJ: Lawrence Erlbaum Associates, Inc.

Bretherton, I., & Mulholland, K. A. (1999). Internal working models in attachment relations: A construct revisited. In J. Cassidy & P. R. Shaver (Eds.), *Handbook of attachment: Theory, research and clinical applications* (pp. 89–111). New York: Guilford.

Carton, J. S., & Carton, E. R. (1998). Nonverbal maternal warmth and children's locus of control of reinforcement. *Journal of Nonverbal Behavior, 22,* 77–86.

Cassidy, J., & Shaver, P. R. (1999). *Handbook of attachment: Theory, research and clinical applications.* New York: Guilford.

Dunn, J., Brown, J., & Beardsall, L. (1991). Family talk about feeling states and children's later understanding of others' emotions. *Developmental Psychology, 27,* 448–455.

Engel, S. (1986). *Learning to reminisce: A developmental study of how young children talk about the past.* Unpublished doctoral dissertation, City University of New York.

Farrant, K., & Reese, E. (2000). Attachment security and early mother–child reminiscing: A developmental exploration. Manuscript submitted for publication.

Farrar, M. J., Fasig, L. G., & Welch-Ross, M. K. (1997). Attachment and emotion in autobiographical memory development. *Journal of Experimental Child Psychology, 67,* 389–408.

Fivush, R. (1988). The functions of event memory: Some comments on Nelson and Barsalou. In U. Neisser & E. Winograd (Eds.), *Remembering reconsidered: Ecological and traditional approaches to memory* (pp. 277–282). New York: Cambridge University Press.

Fivush, R. (1991). The social construction of personal narratives. *Merrill-Palmer Quarterly, 37,* 59–82.

Fivush, R. (1993). Developmental perspectives on autobiographical recall. In G. S. Goodman & B. L. Bottoms (Eds.), *Child victims, child witnesses: Understanding and improving testimony* (pp. 1–24). New York: Guilford

Fivush, R. (1994). Constructing narrative, emotion and self in parent–child conversations about the past. In U. Neisser & R. Fivush (Eds.), *The remembering self: Accuracy and construction in the life narrative* (pp. 136–157). New York: Cambridge University Press.

Fivush, R. (1997). Event memory in childhood. In N. Cowan (Ed.), *The development of memory in childhood* (pp. 139–162). Sussex, England: Psychology Press.

Fivush, R. (1998). Gendered narratives: Elaboration, structure and emotion in parent–child reminiscing across the preschool years. In C. P. Thompson, D. J. Herrmann, D. Bruce, J. D. Read, D. G. Payne, & M. P. Toglia (Eds.), *Autobiographical memory: Theoretical and applied perspectives* (pp. 79–104). Mahwah, NJ: Lawrence Erlbaum Associates, Inc.

Fivush, R., Brotman, M., Buckner, J. P., & Goodman, S. (2000). Gender differences in parent–child emotion narratives. *Sex Roles, 42,* 233–254.

Fivush, R., & Fromhoff, F. (1988). Style and structure in mother–child conversations about the past. *Discourse Processes, 11,* 337–355.

Fivush, R., Haden, C., & Reese, E. (1996). Remembering, recounting and reminiscing: The development of autobiographical memory in social context. In D. Rubin (Ed.), *Reconstructing our past: An overview of autobiographical memory* (pp. 341–359). New York: Cambridge University Press.

Han, J. J., Leichtman, M. D., & Wang, Q. (1998). Autobiographical memory in Korean, Chinese, and American children. *Developmental Psychology, 34,* 701–713.

Harley, K., & Reese, E. (1999). Origins of autobiographical memory. *Developmental Psychology, 35,* 1338–1348.

Hudson, J. A. (1986). Memories are made of this: General event knowledge and the developmental of autobiographic memory. In K. Nelson (Ed.), *Event knowledge: Structure and function in development* (pp. 97–118). Hillsdale, NJ: Lawrence Erlbaum Associates, Inc.

Hudson, J. A. (1990). The emergence of autobiographic memory in mother–child conversation. In R. Fivush & J. A. Hudson (Eds.), *Knowing and remembering in young children* (pp. 166–196). New York: Cambridge University Press.

Koren-Karie, N., Oppenheim, D., Haimovich, Z., & Etzion-Carasso, A. (in press). Dialogues of seven-year-olds with their mothers about emotional events: Development of a typology and exploring links to attachment. In R. N. Emde, D. P. Wolf, & D. Oppenheim (Eds.), *Affective meaning making in narratives: Studies with young children.*

Kuebli, J., Butler, S., & Fivush, R. (1995). Mother–child talk about past events: Relations of maternal language and child gender over time. *Cognition and Emotion, 9,* 265–293.

Laible, D. J., & Thompson, R. A. (2000). Mother–child discourse, attachment security, shared positive affect, and early conscience development. *Child Development, 71,* 1424–1440.

Main, M. (1991). Metacognitive knowledge, metacognitive monitoring, and singular (coherent) vs. multiple (incoherent) model of attachment: Findings and directions for future research. In C. M. Parkes, J. Stevenson-Hinde, & P. Marris (Eds.), *Attachment across the life cycle* (pp. 127–159). London: Routledge.

Main, M., Kaplan, K., & Cassidy, J. (1985). Security in infancy, childhood and adulthood: A move to the level of representation. *Growing points of attachment theory and research. Monographs of the Society for Research in Child Development, 50*(1–2, Serial No. 209), 66–104.

McCabe, A., & Peterson, C. (1991). Getting the story: A longitudinal study of parental styles in eliciting narratives and developing narrative skill. In A. McCabe & C. Peterson (Eds.), *Developing narrative structure* (pp. 217–253). Hillsdale, NJ: Lawrence Erlbaum Associates, Inc.

Mullen, M., & Yi, S. (1995). The cultural context of talk about the past: Implications for the development of autobiographical memory. *Cognitive Development, 10,* 407–419.

Nelson, K. (1986). *Event knowledge: Structures and function in development.* Hillsdale, NJ: Lawrence Erlbaum Associates, Inc.

Nelson, K. (1993). The psychological and social origins of autobiographical memory. *Psychological Science, 1,* 1–8.

Nelson, K. (1996). *Language in cognitive development: Emergence of the mediated mind*. New York: Cambridge University Press.

Nelson, K., & Fivush, R. (2000). The socialization of memory. In E. Tulving & F. Craik (Eds.), *The Oxford handbook of memory* (pp. 283–296). London: Oxford University Press.

Nelson, K., & Gruendel, J. M. (1981). Generalized event representations: Basic building blocks of cognitive development. In M. E. Lamb & A. L. Brown (Eds.), *Advances in development psychology* (Vol. 1, pp. 131–158). Hillsdale, NJ: Lawrence Erlbaum Associates, Inc.

Nelson, K., & Ross, G. (1980). The generalities and specific of long-term memory in infants and young children. In M. Perlmutter (Ed.), *New directions for child development: Children's memory* (pp. 87–101). San Francisco: Jossey-Bass.

Peterson, C., & Bell, M. (1996). Children's memory for traumatic injury. *Child Development, 67*, 3045–3070.

Pillemer, D. (1998). What is remembered about early childhood events? *Clinical Psychology Review, 18*, 895–913.

Reese, E., Haden, C. A., & Fivush, R. (1993). Mother–child conversations about the past: Relationships of style and memory over time. *Cognitive Development, 8*, 403–430.

Reese, E., Haden, C., & Fivush, R. (1996). Mothers, father, daughters, sons: Gender differences in reminiscing. *Research on Language and Social Interaction, 29*, 27–56.

Soloman, J., & George, C. (1999). The measurement of attachment security in infancy and childhood. In J. Cassidy & P. R. Shaver (Eds.), *Handbook of attachment: Theory, research and clinical applications* (pp. 287–317). New York: Guilford.

Teti, D., & McGourty, S. (1996). Using mothers vs. trained observers in assessing children's secure base behavior: Theoretical and methodological considerations. *Child Development, 67*, 597–605.

Thompson, R. (2000). The legacy of early attachments. *Child Development, 71*, 145–152.

van Ijzendoorn, M. H., & Sagi, A. (1999). Cross-cultural patterns of attachment: Universal and contextual dimensions. In J. Cassidy & P. R. Shaver (Eds.), *Handbook of attachment: Theory, research and clinical applications* (pp. 713–734). New York: Guilford.

Waters, E. (1987). Attachment behavior Q-set (Version 3.0) [Computer software]. Stony Brook, NY: State University of New York at Stony Brook, Department of Psychology.

Waters, H. S., Rodriguez, L. M., & Ridgeway, D. (1998). Cognitive underpinnings of narrative attachment assessment. *Journal of Experimental Child Psychology, 71*, 211–234.

JOURNAL OF COGNITION AND DEVELOPMENT, 3(1), 91–115
Copyright © 2002, Lawrence Erlbaum Associates, Inc.

The Best Laid Plans ... :
Beyond Scripts are Counterscripts

Joan M. Lucariello
Lynch School of Education
Boston College

Catherine Mindolovich
The Mount Sinai School of Medicine

This study examined whether *counterscripts* (general, semantic knowledge structures for unexpected events exhibiting definable, common event structure) are part of our event knowledge. Classic among counterscript events are situationally ironic ones (e.g., an agent's goal-directed actions yield the opposite outcome or are superseded by fluke actions in securing a goal). In a category ratings task, adults rated 3 event kinds for ironic status: script (expected, routine events associated with general knowledge structures), counterscript ironic, and anomaly–unexpected (unexpected events with no common structure and not associated with general knowledge structures). The data indicate that general, semantic knowledge structures exist for counterscript ironic events. These events were rated in the ironic range and more ironic than script and anomaly–unexpected events. Script events were rated least ironic. Script and counterscript events emerged as independent event factors. Moreover, counterscript ironic events exhibited internal structure (degree of irony varied across event kinds), a component of conceptual coherence.

In our everyday sociocultural experience, we encounter many kinds of events. Some are commonplace, expected events, such as going to the movies, grocery store, restaurant, dentist, or birthday party. We also experience unexpected events. For example, our best-laid plans might completely backfire on us, yielding the opposite result. Or we might bump into an old elementary school classmate, known for being clumsy, and discover to our utter amazement that she is now a prima ballerina in a major dance company. Or we may get a flat tire on the way to a restau-

---

Requests for reprints should be sent to Joan Lucariello, Boston College, Lynch School of Education, Campion 239E, Chestnut Hill, MA 02467. E-mail: lucariel@bc.edu

rant or attend a birthday party at which a fight erupts. In cognitive psychology and cognitive developmental psychology, considerable attention has been directed to how we learn about and represent expected, commonplace events. To date, however, study of our knowledge about unexpected events is rather limited. For example, it is not known whether we acquire general, semantic knowledge representations for such events. Furthermore, if we do, is this the case for all kinds of unexpected events or for only some and why? These are the questions to be addressed in this research.

We represent commonplace, expected events through general, semantic knowledge structures known as *scripts* (Schank & Abelson, 1977). Scripts were first described by Schank and Abelson (1977) as

> A structure that describes appropriate sequences of events in a particular context. A script is made up of slots and requirements about what can fill those slots. The structure is an interconnected whole, and what is in one slot affects what can be in another. Scripts handle stylized everyday situations. They are not subject to much change, nor do they provide the apparatus for handling totally novel situations. Thus, a script is a predetermined, stereotyped sequence of actions that defines a well-known situation. (p. 41)

Scripts are a major knowledge organization for adults (Bower, Black, & Turner, 1979; Galambos & Rips, 1982; Graesser, Gordon, & Sawyer, 1979; Graesser, Woll, Kowalski, & Smith, 1980; Hue & Erickson, 1991; Schank & Abelson, 1977). Moreover, scripts can be acquired by young children, beginning as early as 2 years of age, and they are a predominant knowledge structure for children (Bauer & Mandler, 1990, 1992; Bauer, Wenner, Dropik, & Wewerka, 2000; Nelson, 1986; Nelson & Gruendel, 1981; Ratner, Smith, & Dion, 1986).

Heretofore, attempts to understand our knowledge of unexpected events have relied on the script structure. In some cases of script–deviant occurrences, these are assimilated and regularized within script organization. For instance, in recall, missing actions and missing goals of an event are inferred by children (Hudson & Nelson, 1983) and scrambled action sequences are restored to canonical order by adults (Bower et al., 1979) and children (Hudson & Nelson, 1983).

In other cases of script–deviant occurrences, these are not absorbed within script organization but related to it. On both the script pointer plus tag (SP + T) model (Schank & Abelson, 1977) and the highly similar schema copy plus tag model (SC + T; Graesser et al., 1979; Graesser et al., 1980; Smith & Graesser, 1981), atypical actions were proposed to be stored as organizational units separate from the script. On these models, in comprehending story texts, a specific memory representation is constructed for each activity. The specific memory representation is believed to contain a *script pointer,* which is a single memory link to the generic script that best fits the activity. The representation also contains tagged actions that are unrelated or inconsistent with the content of the script. The generic script inter-relates the various typical actions as a whole. In contrast, each inconsistent, atypi-cal, or unrelated action is tagged as a functionally separate organizational unit. Atypical unrelated actions are defined as items such as putting a pen in one's pocket or picking a napkin off the floor in the restaurant script (Graesser et al., 1979; Graesser et al.,1980; Smith & Graesser, 1981).

Recall of such *script-irrelevant (unrelated)* atypical actions is initially better than that for typical actions, but atypical actions are forgotten at a faster rate than typical actions (Graesser et al., 1980; Smith & Graesser, 1981). This is due to the importance of the generic script structure in directing recall. The longer the reten-tion interval, the more retrieval becomes dependent on the generic schema. Hence, the actions that are central to the script will persist longer in recall than will the tagged atypical actions, which are less central to the generic script.

It turns out, however, that atypical actions that are script relevant can be quite memorable. Atypical actions that are *script interruptions,* this is, affect the causal flow of events, can be well recalled (Bower et al., 1979). Better recall has been found for script interruptions, such as obstacles and distractions, than for script ac-tions and script irrelevancies (Bower et al., 1979). Obstacles refer to a missing en-abling condition for an imminent action (e.g., you cannot read the French menu). Distractions refer to unexpected events that set up new goals for the actor, taking the actor outside the script temporarily or permanently (e.g., the waiter spills soup on the customer, initiating a trip to the restroom for clean up). Similar results have been found with children (Hudson, 1988). Disruptions (interruptions), such as ob-stacles and distractions, particularly those that are goal related (e.g., block the completion of the goal of an event) were better recalled by children than script ac-tions and script irrelevancies. Data such as these extended the SP + T model to in-clude the goal relevance of the atypical–tagged action as a factor in its recall.

Moreover, others have found the disruption effect to operate with respect to dis-tractions and not obstacles (Davidson & Jergovic, 1996). Furthermore, distractions that led to emotional consequences (e.g., dropping a carton of eggs in the grocery store) were better recalled than distractions that did not (e.g., dropping apples in the grocery store). Emotional consequences led to the agent or others being upset. This research also modified the SP + T model in claiming that not all tags–atypical actions are tagged in the same manner and with the same strength to the schema–script. Factors that combine with the disruption effect, such as emotional-ity, were found to be important in recall of atypical actions.

Although tag models account relatively well for recall patterns for some types of atypical actions in events, we suggest that some types of deviations are better conceived as a category separate from scripts. In particular, we suggest that some script interruptions are so profound and so memorable as to be of equal status to script structures themselves. Furthermore, given that certain kinds of script-rele-vant atypical actions are highly memorable, those unexpected experiences largely based on elaborations of such atypicalities might be among those likely to constitute event structures themselves. In this article, we introduce the concept of *counterscript events* as atypical events that exhibit definable and shared structural characteristics and, hence, as events for which we acquire general, semantic knowledge representations. These representations may be termed *counterscripts*. We focus in particular on the class or category of counterscript events known as "situationally ironic" events (Lucariello, 1994; Lucariello & Mindolovich, 1995; Muecke, 1969). As defined by Lucariello (1994; Lucariello & Mindolovich, 1995), situationally ironic events are events that end contrary or opposite to expectation in highly specified and culturally recognized ways. These ways distinguish ironic events from other anomalous, unexpected events.

To better understand the distinctions among script, counterscript ironic, and anomalous–unexpected events, the structure of events must be analyzed. To that end, four aspects of event structure are discerned: causal relations, emotive structure, person relations, and interpersonal relationships, and temporal–spatial relations. These four aspects of event structure are instantiated differently across scripts and counterscripts (see Table 1).

In script representations, causal relations are based in an agent who undertakes appropriate, goal-directed actions, which achieve the goal. An essential feature of script knowledge is that causal relations are successful. With respect to the second aspect of event structure, emotive structure, scripts embrace a positive–happy emotive structure relative to the agent or agents. This is the result of the successful causal relations wherein agents achieve their goals. Person and interpersonal relations constitute another aspect of event structure. In script structure, person relations exhibit concordance. Agents perform actions and have goals consistent with their identity, traits, roles, and so on. For example, the waitress takes the order and brings the food. Moreover, interpersonal relationships are contingent and reciprocal. The waitress does those things; the diner orders and eats. Finally, as to the fourth aspect of event structure, temporal–spatial relations, scripts represent discrete or delimited time–place contexts. Script events occur, for example, at a restaurant, school, grocery store, or birthday party.

Each of these aspects of event structure can take on other values. It is these other values that produce or result in counterscript events. Many counterscript ironic events are based on aberrant (from script) causal relations. This is not surprising because among the more memorable script-relevant atypical actions are disruptions of the causal flow of events (Bower et al., 1979; Hudson, 1988). The importance of the hierarchical organization representing the goal structure of events is indicated in event recall as well. The causal structure of events has been found to influence the amount of information reported (Ratner et al., 1986; see also Trabasso & Stein, 1996; Trabasso, van den Broek, & Suh, 1989, on the import of causal relations in stories and events).

TABLE 1

Event Structure for Sociocultural Events by Event Kind

			Event Structure		
Event Kinds	Causal Relations	Emotive Structure	Person Relations and Interpersonal Relationships	Temporal–Spatial Relations	Example
Script	$A_g- > G_o- > Act- > Out_W$	Positive–happy	Concordance reciprocity	Discrete–delimited time–place context	Mary is having a birthday party. Her friends have come and brought gifts. She opens her presents, blows out the candles, and they eat cake. They play games and then the kids go home.
Counterscripts Fluke–win	$A_g- > G_o- > Act- > Out_L- >$ Non-G_o Act– > Out$_W$	Positive–happy	Concordance	Discrete–delimited time–place context	Clown practices his trick, where cream pie hits him in face. At show, the trick doesn't work and the kids boo him. Clown sadly walks away, when he slips on the cream into a bucket of water. Kids think that's great and cheer the clown.

(continued)

95

TABLE 1 (Continued)

	Event Structure				
Event Kinds	Causal Relations	Emotive Structure	Person Relations and Interpersonal Relationships	Temporal–Spatial Relations	Example
Planned–loss	$A_g -> G_o -> Act-> $ self-inflicted Out_L	Negative–sad	Concordance	Discrete–delimited time–place context	Billy gets a telescope at his birthday. He wants to be sure nothing happens to it so he leaves his party to put it in his closet. On the way, he trips and falls, breaking it.
Deserved–loss	$A_g ->$ "evil" G_o (Bad G_o/Out for other) $-> Out_L$ for self	Negative–angry	Indeterminate	Discontinuous: not time–place delimited	Cindy won't let Sally play jump rope with her and her friends because she says Sally is clumsy. Then Cindy trips and falls.
Fruitless win–double outcome	$A_g -> G_o -> Act-> Out_L ->$ Out now irrelevant $->$ Out attainable$_{L \& w}$	Negative–sad Negative–sad	Concordance	Discrete–delimited time–place context	The Smiths wake to a great day and decide to have a picnic. They do lots of preparing and then go all the way to the park. Just then clouds come and it starts storming. They drive home. Then the sky clears and the sun comes out.

	$A_g- > G_o- > Act- > Outw- > $ Same $G_o/Act- > Out_L$	Positive–happy–> negative–sad	Concordance	Discontinuous: not time–place delimited	
Instrumental–double outcome		Positive–happy–> negative–sad	Concordance	Discontinuous: not time–place delimited	James Fixx became a famous health and exercise expert through jogging. Later he had a heart attack while jogging and died.
Temporal–imbalance	—	—	Mismatch	Discontinuous: not time–place delimited	Clumsiest child grows up to be prima ballerina.
Contextual–imbalance	—	—	Mismatch	Discontinuous: not time–place delimited	The playground bully, mean to all, is so scared of heights he cries on the jungle gym.
Doomed agent–dramatic	Misinformed $A_g- > G_o- > Act- > Outw = Out_L$	Negative–sad	Concordance	Discontinuous: not time–place delimited	Jimmy is new in town. He trades his best, favorite marbles to kids he meets at the park to make friends. They like him. Then he finds out they don't live around there; they are only visiting.

Note. A_g = agent; G_o = goal; Act = goal-based actions; Out = outcome (win or loss).

One counterscript ironic event kind based on aberrant (from script) causal relations is the "loss" kind (also see Lucariello, 1994; Lucariello & Mindolovich, 1995; Lucariello, Mindolovich, & LeDonne, 2002, for descriptions of these various ironic event kinds). For example, *planned-loss* ironic events refer to the backfired plan. The agent has a goal and takes appropriate actions. Rather than securing the intended outcome, as in script causal relations, these actions achieve the outcome opposite to that intended. The result is that the loss outcome is also self-inflicted. In the Table 1 example, the boy is putting his new telescope away for safekeeping from others and in so doing breaks it himself.

With respect to emotive structure, many of the counterscript ironic events that exhibit script-aberrant causal relations, accordingly exhibit script-aberrant emotive structure. This consists in negative–sad emotion relative to the agent or agents. The importance of script-deviant emotion in memory for atypical actions has already been demonstrated. Memorable disruptions included those leading to more potential consequences, particularly emotional ones, for the actors (Davidson & Jergovic, 1996). In planned-loss, naturally the agent whose plan has backfired is feeling negatively or sadly.

Because aberrations from script structure in both the causal flow of events and in emotional consequences for the agent were among the more memorable script-relevant atypical actions (Bower et al., 1979; Davidson & Jergovic, 1996; Hudson, 1988), it would be expected that the varieties of counterscript ironic events based on elaborations of these disruptions would be the most prototypical ironic event kinds. Loss events are of this variety (so too are double outcome events, which are described later).

A different variety of counterscript ironic events diverge from script structure in terms of the last two event structure features in interaction. "Imbalance" counterscript ironic events exhibit script aberrant temporal–spatial relations in conjunction with person relations. They capture contradiction in person relations, such as agent–action or agent–goal, across contexts. In temporal-imbalance, person relations are contradicted across distinct temporal contexts, generally past versus present (e.g., the clumsy classmate who becomes the prima ballerina). Imbalance counterscript ironic events are likely less prototypical instances of ironic events than are loss events, such as planned-loss. As noted, the latter are based on elaborations of the highly memorable script-aberrant causal relations and emotive structure.

Counterscript events may be distinguished from other unexpected, script-aberrant events that do not qualify as counterscript events. Some nonscript events exhibit idiosyncratic anomalies. They show no common instantiation of event structure. For example, in a deviation of the planned-loss example (in Table 1), let us say that while the boy is putting his telescope away for safekeeping, he does not drop it. Rather, he has to run back to his party because his friends are fighting. In this case, an anomalous, nonscript event has occurred. However, a counterscript ironic event has not. Presumably, we do not acquire general, semantic representations for these events.

To better understand the structure of long-term event memory, it is important to determine if our experience of at least some unexpected events—counterscript events—leads to acquisition of event structures called counterscripts. This possibility contrasts with the view of long-term event knowledge proposed in the SP + T model. Therein only one kind of event knowledge structure exists. This would be the script structure, which captures our understanding of expected, commonplace events. Knowledge of atypical experiences, such as counterscript and anomaly events, would be specified in only tagged units linking to generic scripts. Alternatively, as proposed here, two tiers of event knowledge structures—scripts and counterscripts—would constitute our event knowledge. Moreover, on this view, experience with anomalous events would not lead to acquisition of generic, semantic event knowledge structures.

In this research, we set out to determine if general, semantic event knowledge structures exist for one kind of nonscript-like unexpected event kind, the *situationally ironic* event. Adult understanding of counterscript ironic events, in relation to script and anomalous events, was explored. Whether events defined as counterscript ironic, based on their event structure features, were understood (rated) as such, and distinctively so, by adults was assessed.

The study of adult understanding of counterscript ironic events is prerequisite to the study of children's acquisition of such. These event structures must first be operationalized. This is done in this research. These event structures must also be validated; that is, verified through judgements other than those of the investigators. Only if counterscript ironic structures were demonstrated, would one then explore when and how children acquire them.

Eight counterscript ironic event structures were studied (see Table 1). These represented the five ironic event kinds, and within these the particular subkinds, found to be the more prototypical instances of ironical situations (Lucariello, 1994). Of the eight studied here, five are based on script-aberrant causal relations. Of these, the most similar to script event structure are "wins," events of which a major type is *fluke-win*. In these events, inadvertent, nongoal-directed actions, rather than goal-directed ones, secure the outcome. Such is the aberrancy in causal relations. Nonetheless, the intended goal is achieved in the outcome, making these events very similar to script events. Moreover, because the desired outcome is attained, the emotive structure of fluke-win counterscript events is, similar to that of scripted events, positive–happy.

The remaining four counterscript ironic event kinds based on script-aberrant causal relations lead to loss outcomes. Hence, they exhibit script-contradictory, negative–sad emotive structure as well. "Loss" event kinds entail a single loss outcome. The planned-loss form already described is a major type of loss. A second type is *deserved-loss*. In these events, an agent has an inappropriate goal, that of desiring or causing a loss for another. The agent may even take action to achieve that goal. The outcome, however, is that the agent becomes recipient of a loss instead or as well. Such events depict "poetic justice" situations. The third and fourth forms are two "double outcome" ironic event kinds. Double outcome events entail two opposing outcomes, win and loss. In *fruitless win–double outcome* events, the agent has a goal and takes appropriate actions, but the outcome is lost (not achieved). Subsequently, when the outcome is no longer relevant or desired, it becomes attainable. This final outcome constitutes a bittersweet experience. It represents a loss because it arrived too late, but it reminds one of the win it could have been. In *instrumental–double outcome* counterscript ironic events, the very means (goal and actions) to winning become the means to losing. Think here of the role of jogging in the life of James Fixx. He became famous for his jogging-based activities and subsequently suffered a fatal heart attack while jogging.

Two additional counterscript ironic kinds studied are "imbalance events," which exhibit script aberrant temporal–spatial relations in conjunction with person relations. They capture contradiction in person relations, such as agent–action or agent–goal, across contexts. These contexts can be temporal (as in the temporal-imbalance form already described) or spatial, as in contextual-imbalance (e.g., the poor banker, the toothless dentist).

The eighth form studied, "dramatic" irony, is associated with literary works and the theater (see Muecke, 1969). The most common type has been defined and dubbed *doomed agent* (Lucariello, 1994). Herein, causal relations are successful: The agent formulates a goal, pursues it with goal-based actions, and attains the desired outcome. However, the agent is operating in a misinformed or uninformed state relative to an observer (e.g., the audience or reader). In light of full, accurate information, the attained outcome is a loss—not a win. One can think of the death of Shakespeare's Romeo here.

This experiment uses a category ratings methodology. The ironic status of three event kinds—script, counterscript ironic, anomaly–unexpected—is assessed. Ratings are along a 7-point scale, affording comparisons across these three event kinds. Exemplars of the eight counterscript events defined here comprise the counterscript ironic events to be rated. To assure that ratings are not instance specific, these eight counterscript kinds are presented in three different thematic contents. The two control event kinds (script and anomaly–unexpected) are constructed to match their counterscript standard; hence, they also appear in the three different thematic contents.

Several findings would reveal a category of counterscript ironic event structures. First, ratings for the eight counterscript ironic events should exhibit a tight range and one that places all these event kinds at the ironic end of the scale. Second, ironic ratings for these events should be distinguishable from the ratings for script events. Indeed, counterscript ironic events and script events should be the two event kinds most differentiable on the ratings. Script events are expected and counterscript events are unexpected in a way that contradicts or opposes script event structure. Accordingly, the rating range for script events should be tight and one that places these events at the least ironic end of the scale. Moreover, if scripts and counterscripts represent two distinct, independent event kinds (categories), each should emerge as a distinct event category or factor. Furthermore, if counterscript ironic events represent a distinct category of unexpected events, their ratings should also be distinguishable from those for anomaly–unexpected events. The latter should receive the less-ironic ratings. Only unexpected events exhibiting specified event structure features, and not all unexpected or script-divergent events, are counterscript ironic.

That a category of counterscript ironic events exists would be supported also by data showing internal structure to this category. Internal structure is one component of conceptual coherence (Medin & Wattenmaker, 1987; Murphy & Medin, 1985). Whether the category of counterscript ironic events—inclusive of all eight counterscript kinds—exhibits internal structure will be assessed by assessing variation in ironic ratings across the eight counterscript ironic kinds. Those kinds based on divergence from scripts in both causal relations and emotive structure (e.g., loss, double outcome) are proposed as the most prototypical ironic event kinds and, hence, should be rated significantly more ironic than less-prototypical kinds (e.g., imbalance).

Finally, ratings for the two control events should also be distinguishable. Anomaly–unexpected events, because they are unexpected, should be viewed as more ironic than script events. The ratings for anomaly events then should generally fall on the scale between the ratings for script and counterscript ironic events.

METHOD

Participants

A total of 48 graduate students recruited from psychology courses participated in this study. They had no prior knowledge of the properties of scripts. The 48 were divided evenly into three groups of 16. Each group rated a separate packet of event stories (see details on packet formation next).

Materials

Events to be rated for counterscript ironic status were presented in story form. Three event kinds were among the to be rated story stimuli. Two were nonironic (control event stories). Nonironic script event stories depicted expected, normative, commonplace events. Nonironic anomaly–unexpected event stories depicted unexpected events, in which this unexpectedness was idiosyncratic; that is, not classifiable as counterscript ironic. The third event kind, counterscript ironic, were stories depicting unexpected events categorizable as ironic.

Twenty-four counterscript ironic event stories were generated. These depicted eight ironic event kinds rendered in three different themes (birthday, circus, and play–park). These eight included: fluke-win, planned-loss, deserved-loss, fruitless win–double outcome, instrumental–double outcome, temporal-imbalance, contextual-imbalance, and doomed agent-dramatic.

Each of these 24 ironic event stories (8 event kinds × 3 themes) was matched by a script control story ($n = 24$) and an anomaly–unexpected control story ($n = 24$). These were identical to their respective ironic standard until their endings. Hence, a total of 72 (24 counter script ironic, 24 script, and 24 anomaly–unexpected) event stories were rated. Three event story stimuli are presented in the Appendix. These represent the three event kinds (counterscript ironic, script, and anomaly–unexpected) in the birthday theme for the planned-loss form.

Three rating packets of 24 event stories each (8 ironic, 8 script, and 8 anomaly–unexpected) were formed. For each packet, for the 8 ironic kinds, two control stories were included and these varied in theme from each other and from the ironic standard with which they were associated (e.g., in Packet 1, were the planned-loss irony story birthday theme, the planned-loss script story circus theme, and the planned-loss anomaly–unexpected story park-play theme). Accordingly, per packet, there were 8 stories in each of the three themes. Stories were ordered randomly in the packets.

Procedure

Each rater was given a packet and told to return it to the experimenters when finished. The following instruction face sheet, modeled after Rosch (1973, 1975), was attached to each packet:

> This study has to do with what we have in mind when we use words which refer to categories. Let's take the word *red* as an example. Close your eyes and imagine a true red. Now imagine an orangish red ... imagine a purple red. Although you might still name the orange red or the purple red with the term *red,* they are not as good examples of red (as clear cases of what *red* refers to) as the clear "true" red. In short, some reds are redder than others. The same is true for other kinds of categories. Think of dogs. You all have some notion of what a "real dog," a "doggy dog" is. To me a retriever or a German shepherd is a very doggy dog while a Pekinese is a less doggy dog. Notice that this kind of judgment has nothing to do with how well you like the thing; you can like a purple red better than a true red but still recognize that the color you like is not a true red. You may prefer to own a Pekinese without

thinking that it is the breed that best represents what people mean by dogginess.

The instructions continued, asking participants to judge how good an example of the category irony (ironical situations) various instances of the category are. Ratings were done on a 7-point scale, ranging from 1 (*very good example*) to 7 (*very poor/not an example*).

RESULTS

Comparability of Three Ratings Groups

To assess comparability of the three ratings groups, means for each of the three event story kinds (counterscript ironic, script, and anomaly–unexpected) were tabulated per packet. In each packet, for each participant, the eight ratings for the eight event stories representing each of the three event kinds were tallied and divided by eight to obtain a mean for each event kind. Packet means for event story kind were then tabulated by summing across the 16 scores (each participant's mean rating for event story kind) and dividing by 16 (the total number of participants).

Mean ratings for the same event kind were compared across packet using three one-way analyses of variance (ANOVAs). No differences in mean rating across packet were found for counterscript ironic events, $F(2, 45) = .027$, and script events, $F(2, 45) = .376$. A significant difference was found in mean ratings for the anomaly–unexpected events across packets, $F(2, 45) = 5.84, p < .006$. Post hoc tests (Bonferroni) showed no difference in ratings across Packets 1 (packet $M = 5.58, SD = 0.74$) and 2 (packet $M = 5.52, SD = 0.82$). However, the anomaly–unexpected events in Packet 3 (packet $M = 4.66, SD = 0.98$) were rated more ironic than those events in Packet 1, $p < .01$, and Packet 2, $p < .02$.

Because no differences were found in the mean ratings for both script and counterscript event kinds across packets, these packet means will not be considered further. Although differences in the mean ratings for anomaly–unexpected events were found across some packets, as we will see later, these are of no consequence.

Comparisons of Overall Mean Ratings of Three Event Kinds

Overall means (collapsing across packets) per event story kind (counterscript ironic, script, and anomaly–unexpected) were obtained by tallying the means for each of the 48 participants per event kind and dividing by 48. A repeated measures ANOVA was run on these overall means, with the three event kinds as a within-subjects factor.

These means differed significantly, $F(2, 94) = 203.14, p < .000$. Paired sample tests across the means show statistically significant differences across all event kind comparisons. Counterscript ironic events ($M = 3.13, SD = 0.97$) were rated significantly more ironic than both anomaly–unexpected events ($M = 5.26, SD = 0.94$), $t(47) = -14.05, p < .000$, and script events ($M = 6.38, SD = 0.81$), $t(47) = 17.86, p < .000$. Moreover, script events were rated less ironic than anomaly–unexpected events, $t(47) = 7.21, p < .000$.

Even in Packet 3 (in which the mean for the anomaly–unexpected events was more ironic than for these events in Packets 1 and 2), all event kinds were rated significantly different from one another. Counterscript ironic events ($M = 3.09, SD = 0.91$) were rated significantly more ironic than both anomaly–unexpected events ($M = 4.66, SD = 0.98$), $t(15) = -7.22, p < .000$, and script events ($M = 6.24, SD = 1.16$), $t(15) = -9.54, p < .000$; script events were rated significantly less ironic than anomaly–unexpected events, $t(15) = -4.80, p < .000$.

Mean Ratings for Eight Specific Event Types Within the Three Event Kinds

Having already computed the overall mean ratings for each of the three event kinds (previously), the mean ratings by the eight specific event types within kind can also be computed. Accordingly, the overall mean rating (collapsing over theme) for each of the eight counterscript ironic event kinds and their respective anomaly and script control event kinds was calculated. Overall means per counterscript kind were calculated by adding the score (rating) assigned to each (e.g., planned-loss) by the 48 participants and dividing the total score by 48. The same procedure was followed for calculating overall means for the eight anomaly and eight script control event kinds, corresponding to the eight counterscript event kinds. These data are reported in Table 2 (means by theme are available from Joan M. Lucariello).

Overall mean ratings for the eight counterscript ironic event kinds placed at the irony end of the scale. The rating range was tight (2.46–3.81). All counterscript ironic kinds were rated between 2 (*pretty good*) and 4 (*moderate*) examples of ironical situations. The rating range for script events was tight (5.86–6.73) and was at the extreme least ironic end of the scale. No script control event was rated better than a poor to very poor/not an example of a counterscript ironic event. The rating range for anomaly–unexpected events was 4.51 to 6.42. These events were rated from moderate to poor/not an example exemplars of ironical situations.

Category Structure

Event kinds (counterscript ironic, script, and anomaly)–unexpected as categories. To determine whether each event kind coheres as a category (whether the eight event types within a kind cohere as a category), an exploratory principal

TABLE 2
Mean Ratings of Three Event Kinds by Form for Goodness as Exemplars
of Counterscript Ironic Events

| | Event Kinds | | | | | |
| | Counterscript Ironic | | Anomaly–Unexpected Nonironic | | Script Nonironic | |
Form	M	SD	M	SD	M	SD
Planned-loss	2.46	1.22	5.07	1.07	5.98	1.00
Fruitless win–double outcome	2.49	0.96	5.15	0.78	6.73	0.33
Fluke-wins	3.05	0.98	4.82	1.12	6.33	0.75
Deserved-loss	3.06	0.86	4.51	1.13	6.60	0.57
Doomed agent–dramatic	3.08	1.19	5.00	1.29	6.73	0.46
Instrumental–double outcome	3.42	1.32	5.10	0.88	6.71	0.44
Contextual-imbalance	3.61	0.88	6.10	0.73	5.86	0.86
Temporal-imbalance	3.81	0.97	6.42	0.52	6.10	0.62

axis factor analysis (varimax rotation) of the 72 event stories was conducted for three factors. It was expected that all the script events would load on a script factor and that all the counterscript ironic events would load on a counterscript factor. For anomaly–unexpected events, although it was expected that these might load on an anomaly–unexpected event factor, because this event kind is not presumed to map onto an underlying event category, one would not expect this factor to be strong. That is, all such events might not be expected to load on this factor. Use of the Scree Test (Cattell, 1966) clearly suggest three factors (see Table 3).

The first factor was labeled script events because seven of eight script control event kinds (21 of 24 script event stories) had high loadings, ranging from .58 to .78, on Factor 1. The second factor was labeled counterscript ironic events because six of eight counterscript ironic event kinds (18 of 24 counterscript event stories) loaded on Factor 2 with generally high loadings: .36 to .66. Moreover, the counterscript event kind with the weakest loading (.22) on Factor 2—instrumental–double outcome—did not cross load on either of the other factors. Finally, Factor 3 was labeled anomaly–unexpected events. Three of eight control events of this kind (nine anomaly–unexpected event stories) had high loadings on Factor 3. Three additional anomaly–unexpected control event kinds (nine anomaly–unexpected event stories) loaded on Factor 2, the counterscript event factor. One additional anomaly control event kind loaded on Factor 1, the script event factor.

Only one of the eight event kinds for each of its three event kinds (counterscript, script, and anomaly–unexpected) did not distribute as hypothesized. These were all associated with the contextual-imbalance form—the factor loadings are rendered at the bottom of Table 3. All contextual-imbalance event stories—hence, its

TABLE 3
Loadings of Ratings for 72 Events by Three Event Kinds

Events	Factor 1: Script	Factor 2: Counterscript	Factor 3: Anomaly– Unexpected
Script (planned-loss)	.78[a]		
Script (deserved-loss)	.77[a]		
Script (temporal-imbalance)	.72[a]	.29	
Script (doomed agent-dramatic)	.70[a]		
Script (instrumental–double outcome)	.67[a]		
Script (fluke-wins)	.63[a]	–.22	
Script (fruitless win–double outcome)	.58[a]		
Anomaly (temporal-imbalance)	.34		.24
Counterscript (planned-loss)		.66[a]	
Counterscript (temporal-imbalance)		.61[a]	
Counterscript (doomed agent-dramatic)		.59[a]	
Anomaly (planned-loss)		.42	
Anomaly (doomed agent-dramatic)		.40	
Counterscript (deserved-loss)		.39[a]	
Counterscript (fluke-wins)		.36[a]	
Anomaly (deserved-loss)		.35	
Counterscript (instrumental–double outcome)		.22[a]	
Anomaly (instrumental–double outcome)			.81[a]
Anomaly (fruitless win–double outcome)	.20		.80[a]
Anomaly (fluke-wins)	.28		.52[a]
Counterscript (fruitless win–double outcome)			.40
Script (contextual-imbalance)			–.42
Counterscript (contextual-imbalance)			.21
Anomaly (contextual-imbalance)	.25		–.26

[a]Hypothesized factor loadings.

three counterscript ironic, three anomaly–unexpected, and three script event stories—loaded on Factor 3. The three anomaly–unexpected event stories also cross loaded on Factor 1.

Internal structure of counterscript event category. To determine whether counterscript ironic event kinds differ in their degree of irony, dependent *t* tests were used to make selected pairwise comparisons on the overall mean ratings (see Table 2) for some counterscript ironic event kinds. Two varieties of counterscript ironic event kinds were proposed to be represented among the eight kinds studied. One variety was based on script-aberrant causal relations and emotive structure (loss, double outcome); the second variety was based on deviation from script structure in terms of temporal–spatial relations in conjunction with person relations (imbalance). To establish within-variety similarity, paired comparisons of the mean ratings for all event kinds within each of these two varieties were conducted. This makes for seven comparisons. The expectation is for no significant differences in mean irony ratings for the counterscript ironic event kinds within each of the two varieties.

It was proposed, in addition, that the script-aberrant causal and emotive variety would be the more prototypical instances of the category of counterscript ironic event kinds. The data on mean ratings per ironic kind (see Table 2) suggest this to be the case. Planned-loss and fruitless win–double outcome were the two most ironic event kinds based on mean ratings, whereas temporal- and contextual-imbalances had the lowest mean ratings. Accordingly, a second set of paired comparisons compares the mean ratings of event kinds across these two varieties of counterscript ironic event kinds. Mean ratings of each of the four causally and emotively aberrant counterscript kinds (planned-loss, deserved-loss, fruitless win–double outcome, and instrumental–double outcome) were compared with mean ratings for each of the two temporally–spatially, in conjunction with person relations, aberrant forms (contextual- and temporal-imbalance). Hence, eight comparisons were made.

Because 15 pairwise comparisons were done in total, the alpha level for significance is $p < .003$. The data appear in Table 4. Comparisons of the mean irony ratings of counterscript ironic events within each of the two varieties—causal and emotive aberrations and temporal–spatial in conjunction with person relations aberrations—showed no significant differences. Across variety comparisons showed

TABLE 4
Comparison of Mean Ratings for Select Counterscript Ironic Event Kinds

Comparison	t value	df	Significance ($p < .003$)
Within-kind comparisons			
Planned-loss versus fruitless win–double outcome	−0.11	15	$p < .92$
Planned-loss versus deserved-loss	−2.24	15	$p < .04$
Planned-loss versus instrumental–double outcome	−3.01	15	$p < .01$
Fruitless win–double outcome versus deserved loss	−2.32	15	$p < .04$
Fruitless win–double outcome versus instrumental–double outcome	−2.64	15	$p < .02$
Deserved-loss versus instrumental–double outcome	−1.25	15	$p < .23$
Contextual-imbalance versus temporal-imbalance	−0.55	15	$p < .59$
Across-kind comparisons			
Planned-loss versus contextual-imbalance	−4.19	15	$p < .001$[a]
Planned-loss versus temporal-imbalance	−3.25	15	$p < .005$
Fruitless win–double outcome versus contextual-imbalance	−4.56	15	$p < .000$[a]
Fruitless win–double outcome versus temporal-imbalance	−3.73	15	$p < .002$[a]
Deserved-loss versus contextual-imbalance	−3.08	15	$p < .01$
Deserved-loss versus temporal-imbalance	−2.14	15	$p < .05$
Instrumental–double outcome versus contextual-imbalance	−0.70	15	$p < .50$
Instrumental–DO versus temporal-imbalance	−0.95	15	$p < .36$

[a]Significant comparison.

two of the four causal and emotive script-aberrant event kinds to be rated more ironic than those event kinds based in script–deviant, temporal–spatial relations in conjunction with person relations. Specifically, fruitless win–double outcome events were rated more ironic than temporal- and contextual-imbalances. Planned-loss events were rated more ironic than contextual-imbalance events, and there was a trend for planned-loss events to be rated more ironic than temporal-imbalance events.

DISCUSSION

The aim of this research was to determine if general, semantic event knowledge structures exist for one kind of nonscript, unexpected event known as situationally ironic events (Lucariello, 1994; Lucariello & Mindolovich, 1995). The common structure of these events was defined here. Due to their shared structural characteristics, these events were thought to be learned. The concept of counterscripts was introduced to refer to event knowledge structures that are acquired for those unexpected events exhibiting systematic and common event structure. Situationally ironic events were considered a key category of counterscript events. Such events may be distinguished from anomalous, idiosyncratic unexpected events. These do not exhibit a systematic or common event structure. Accordingly, general, semantic knowledge structures are not thought to be acquired for such events.

These data are consistent with the suggestion that there are general, semantic event knowledge structures for situationally ironic events. Hence, counterscript representations may form part of our event knowledge. All eight counterscript ironic event kinds attained overall mean ratings on the ironic end of the scale. They were rated as pretty good to moderate exemplars of ironical situations. Moreover, counterscript ironic events were rated most ironic among the three event kinds. As expected, script events were rated least ironic. Counterscript ironic events and script events should be most highly differentiable from one another. Script events are expected and counterscript events are unexpected in ways that contradict or oppose script event structure. Hence, the rating range for script events was tight and one that placed these events at the least ironic end of the scale. In addition, counterscript events formed a distinct category among unexpected events. They were rated more ironic than anomaly–unexpected events. Only unexpected events exhibiting specified event structure features, and not all unexpected or script-divergent events, are counterscript ironic. Anomaly–unexpected events, however, were rated more ironic than script events. Because anomaly–unexpected events are unexpected, they should be viewed as more ironic than script events.

Furthermore, counterscripts emerged, as did scripts, as a separate event factor in the factor analysis. Seven of the eight script event kinds had high loadings on Factor 1. Six of the eight counterscript ironic event kinds had strong or exclusive loadings (or both) on Factor 2. The anomaly–unexpected events did not load as clearly on one factor. Three of seven anomaly–unexpected event kinds had high loadings on the third factor. Three others loaded on Factor 2 (the counterscript factor). Because anomaly–unexpected events are not thought to tap general, semantic knowledge structures, it was not expected that they would emerge as a strong or single factor. That some anomaly–unexpected events should load on the counterscript factor would be expected. Anomaly–unexpected events are structurally and definitionally closer to counterscript, than script events, because both are unexpected events.

   That general, semantic event knowledge structures exist for counterscript ironic events is evident in the added finding that such events appear to exhibit internal structure. This is one component of conceptual coherence (Medin & Wattenmaker, 1987; Murphy & Medin, 1985). Prior research has shown that script-relevant atypical actions that were script aberrant in terms of both causal relations (Bower et al., 1979; Hudson, 1988) and emotional consequences (Davidson & Jergovic, 1996) were highly memorable. The saliency of these aberrations suggests that the variety of counterscript ironic event kinds based on elaborations of such deviations would be the more prototypical forms. An ordering of these event kinds, from most to least ironic (based on the overall mean per kind; see Table 2) shows this to be the case. The variety exhibiting script-aberrant causal relations and emotive structure ("loss" and "double outcome" events) were rated more ironic than the variety exhibiting script-aberrant temporal–spatial relations in conjunction with person relations ("imbalance" events). The latter were rated least ironic. In comparing the mean ratings across these two varieties, it was the case that two of the former kind—planned-loss and fruitless win–double outcome—were found to be significantly more ironic than contextual-imbalances. In addition, fruitless win–double outcome events were rated significantly more ironic than temporal-imbalance events and planned-loss events approached significance in this regard. The peripherality of contextual-imbalance as a category instance may account for the failure of this counterscript ironic event kind, and its control stories, to load appropriately on the respective factors in the factor analysis. Peripherality could account for indiscriminability across category and noncategory instances. (Alternatively or additionally, some unknown problem with the stimuli depicting these nine events may have been operative.)

   It would seem then that our knowledge of atypical, nonscript fitting events cannot be entirely specified simply as tagged units, as proposed in the SP + T/SC + T models (Graesser et al., 1979; Graesser et al., 1980; Schank & Abelson, 1977; Smith & Graesser, 1981). The hypothesis here that counterscript event representations are event structures in their own right, and hence exist along with scripts as part of our event knowledge base, seems to provide a better fit to the data. Although a direct test comparing the efficacy of the counterscript and tag models in capturing our memory of atypical actions remains to be done, these data point us to the important possibility that long-term event knowledge consists in two event structures: scripts and counterscripts.

This organization of event knowledge in long-term memory has implications for the processing of events. Two event knowledge structures would be available to interpret event experiences, making two processing paths possible. On a serial processing route, scripts would be activated when events are first experienced. If script-based expectations were violated, then knowledge of counterscript events, such as ironic ones, would be activated to interpret the experience. This processing path is similar to that proposed by some for interpreting nonliteral language. Literal meaning is processed first and only when found inconsistent with the context does the hearer seek an alternative, nonliteral meaning (Grice, 1975, 1978; Searle, 1975, 1979). Humor may also be processed serially (Long & Graesser, 1988; Raskin, 1984; Suls, 1972).

On a parallel processing route, both script and counterscript knowledge structures would be accessed when a person experiences events. The counterscript schema would then be activated when the script structure did not account for the experience at hand and the counterscript schema did. Some have challenged the notion of serial processing and proposed a parallel-processing route for humor (Long & Graesser, 1988) and for nonliteral language (Glucksberg, Gildea, & Bookin, 1982). Indeed, in the case of nonliteral language, the serial hypothesis has been challenged by evidence suggesting that listeners do not automatically construct a level of representation solely in terms of the literal meaning of an utterance (Gibbs, 1979, 1983, 1984). This latter processing path may be applicable to the processing of events as well. Scripts may not be automatically retrieved first; that is, before counterscripts. How counterscript event experiences are processed is a subject for future research and may be illuminating for the general debate on serial and parallel processing of humor and nonliteral language.

Given counterscripts as event knowledge structures, important implications for developmental psychology follow. Key among these is how children acquire counterscripts. Clearly, scripts are acquired by very young children (Bauer & Mandler, 1990, 1992; Bauer et al., 2000; Nelson, 1986; Nelson & Gruendel, 1981; Ratner et al., 1986). On the other hand, children as old as 9 years of age seem to have considerable difficulty learning counterscripts (Lucariello & Mindolovich, 1995; Lucariello et al., 2002). Learning of counterscripts seems protracted and effortful.

Counterscript learning is challenging because it entails acquisition of a second tier of event knowledge contradictory to the first scripts (see Gelman & Lucariello, 2002; Lucariello & Mindolovich, 1995; Lucariello et al., 2002, for fuller discussion of counterscript learning). Several cognitive processes underlie learning in which the new knowledge contradicts prior knowledge, which nonetheless is reliable and hence must also be maintained. Prime among these is the cognitive disequilibrium that results from experiencing counterscript events in which the structure contradicts current event knowledge (scripts). This disequilibrium can lead to learning.

Learning requires two highly advanced cognitive processes. One is the principle of "transcendence." To acquire information (counterscripts) that contradicts prior knowledge (scripts), in which the prior knowledge is reliable and hence must also be maintained, a process of transcending prior knowledge must occur. A second cognitive process needed for learning is dialectical metarepresentation. This is reasoning about contradictions in one's own thought and relative to metarepresentations. In learning counterscripts, contradictory tiers of event knowledge must be maintained in the knowledge base. These tiers are the primary representations (scripts) and the secondary, metarepresentations (counterscripts). Operation of these two cognitive processes—transcendence and dialectical metarepresentation—is afforded by the achievement of what might be termed a "skeptical mind." The skeptical mind is one wherein the relativity of one's own knowledge is the foundational operating principle. It consists in the generalizing capacity of our category formation (knowledge acquisition) processes and a concurrent detachment or skeptical orientation toward the adequacy of our general representations or categories. Study of the development of these cognitive processes entailed in counterscript learning is a subject for future research.

In conclusion, our long-term event knowledge appears to consist in two event schematic structures: scripts and counterscripts. Scripts represent our knowledge of expected, commonplace events. Counterscripts represent our knowledge of unexpected (nonscript) events that exhibit specifiable and common event structure. Situationally ironic events are a classic case of counterscript events. As shown in this research, situationally ironic events are ones for which counterscripts are acquired. The existence of two event knowledge structures has implications for how these event structures are accessed in the interpretation of events. It also has implications for development, relative to children's learning of counterscripts and the role of scripts in that learning process.

ACKNOWLEDGMENTS

Portions of this work were presented at the 2001 biennial meeting of the Society for Research in Child Development in Minneapolis, MN.

We are grateful to Patricia Bauer for many important and insightful suggestions that strengthened this research and its presentation. We also wish to thank Larry Ludlow and Rebekah Levine Coley for assistance with data analysis.

REFERENCES

Bauer, P. J., & Mandler, J. M. (1990). Remembering what happened next: Very young children's recall of event sequences. In R. Fivush & J. A. Hudson (Eds.), *Knowing and remembering in young children: Emory symposia in cognition* (Vol. 3, pp. 9–29). New York: Cambridge University Press.

Bauer, P. J., & Mandler, J. M. (1992). Putting the horse before the cart: The use of temporal order in recall of events by one-year-old children. *Developmental Psychology, 28,* 441–452.

Bauer, P. J., Wenner, J. A., Dropik, P. L., & Wewerka, S. S. (2000). Parameters of remembering and forgetting in the transition from infancy to early childhood. *Monographs of the Society for Research in Child Development, 65*(4, Serial No. 263).

Bower, G. H., Black, J. B., & Turner, T. J. (1979). Scripts in memory for text. *Cognitive Psychology, 11,* 177–220.

Cattell, R. B. (1966). The scree test for the number of factors. *Multivariate Behavioral Research, 1,* 140–161.

Davidson, D., & Jergovic, D. (1996). Children's memory for atypical actions in script-based stories: An examination of the disruption effect. *Journal of Experimental Child Psychology, 61,* 134–152.

Galambos, J. A., & Rips, L. J. (1982). Memory for routines. *Journal of Verbal Learning and Verbal Behavior, 21,* 260–281.

Gelman, R., & Lucariello, J. (2002). Learning in cognitive development. In H. Pashler (Series Ed.) & C. R. Gallistel (Vol. Ed.), *Stevens' handbook of experimental psychology: Vol. 3. Learning, motivation, and emotion* (3rd ed.). New York: Wiley.

Gibbs, R. (1979). Contextual effects in understanding indirect requests. *Discourse Processes, 2,* 1–10.

Gibbs, R. (1983). Do people always process the literal meanings of indirect requests? *Journal of Experimental Psychology: Learning, Memory, and Cognition, 9,* 524–533.

Gibbs, R. (1984). Literal meaning and psychological theory. *Cognitive Science, 8,* 275–304.

Glucksberg, S., Gildea, P., & Bookin, H. (1982). On understanding nonliteral speech: Can people ignore metaphors? *Journal of Verbal Learning and Verbal Behavior, 21,* 85–98.

Graesser, A. C., Gordon, S. E., & Sawyer, J. D. (1979). Recognition memory for typical and atypical actions in scripted activities: Tests of a script pointer + tag hypothesis. *Journal of Verbal Learning and Verbal Behavior, 18,* 319–332.

Graesser, A. C., Woll, S. B., Kowalski, D. J., & Smith, D. A. (1980). Memory for typical and atypical actions in scripted activities. *Journal of Experimental Psychology: Human Learning and Memory, 6,* 503–515.

Grice, H. P. (1975). Logic and conversation. In P. Cole & J. Morgan (Eds.), *Syntax and semantics: Vol. 3. Speech acts* (pp. 41–58). New York: Academic.

Grice, H. P. (1978). Some further notes on logic and conversation. In P. Cole (Ed.), *Syntax and semantics: Vol. 9. Pragmatics* (pp. 113–128). New York: Academic.

Hudson, J. (1988).Children's memory for atypical actions in script-based stories: Evidence for a disruption effect. *Journal of Experimental Child Psychology, 46,* 159–173.

Hudson, J., & Nelson, K. (1983). Effects of script structure on children's story recall. *Developmental Psychology, 19,* 625–635.

Hue, C., & Erickson, J. R. (1991). Normative studies of sequence strength and scene structure of 30 scripts. *American Journal of Psychology, 104,* 229–240.

Long, D. L., & Graesser, A. C. (1988). Wit and humor in discourse processing. *Discourse Processes, 11,* 35–60.

Lucariello, J. (1994). Situational irony: A concept of events gone awry. *Journal of Experimental Psychology: General, 123,* 129–145.

Lucariello, J., & Mindolovich, C. (1995). The development of complex metarepresentational reasoning: The case of situational irony. *Cognitive Development, 10,* 551–576.

Lucariello, J., Mindolovich, C., & LeDonne, M. (2002). *Acquiring counterscripts: Achieving a "skeptical mind."* Manuscript in preparation.

Medin, D. L., & Wattenmaker, W. D. (1987). Category cohesiveness, theories, and cognitive archeology. In U. Neisser (Ed.), *Concepts and conceptual development: Ecological and intellectual factors in categorization* (pp. 25–62). Cambridge, England: Cambridge University Press.

Muecke, D. (1969). *The compass of irony*. London: Methuen.

Murphy, G. L., & Medin, D. L. (1985). The role of theories in conceptual coherence. *Psychological Review, 92,* 289–316.

Nelson, K. (Ed.). (1986). *Event knowledge: Structure and function in development*. Hillsdale, NJ: Lawrence Erlbaum Associates, Inc.

Nelson, K., & Gruendel, J. (1981). Generalized event representations: Basic building blocks of cognitive development. In M. E. Lamb & A. L. Brown (Eds.), *Advances in developmental psychology* (Vol. 1, pp. 131–158). Hillsdale, NJ: Lawrence Erlbaum Associates, Inc.

Raskin, V. (1984). *Semantic mechanisms of humor*. Boston: Reidel.

Ratner, H. H., Smith, B. S., & Dion, S. A. (1986). Development of memory for events. *Journal of Experimental Child Psychology, 41,* 411–428.

Rosch, E. (1973). On the internal structure of perceptual and semantic categories. In T. E. Moore (Ed.), *Cognitive development and the acquisition of language* (pp. 111–144). New York: Academic.

Rosch, E. (1975). Cognitive representations of semantic categories. *Journal of Experimental Psychology: General, 104,* 192–233.

Schank, R. C., & Abelson, R. (1977). *Scripts, plans, goals and understanding*. Hillsdale, NJ: Lawrence Erlbaum Associates, Inc.

Searle, J. (1975). Indirect speech acts. In P. Cole & J. Morgan (Eds.), *Syntax and semantics: Vol. 3. Speech acts* (pp. 59–82). New York: Academic.

Searle, J. (1979). Metaphor. In A. Ortony (Ed.), *Metaphor and thought* (pp. 92–123). Cambridge, England: Cambridge University Press.

Smith, D. A., & Graesser, A. C. (1981). Memory for actions in scripted activities as a function of typicality, retention interval, and retrieval task. *Memory & Cognition, 9,* 550–559.

Suls, J. M. (1972). A two-stage model for the appreciation of jokes and cartoons: An information-processing analysis. In J. H. Goldstein & P. E. McGhee (Eds.), *The psychology of humor* (pp. 81–100). New York: Academic.

Trabasso, T., & Stein, N. L. (1996). Narrating, representing, and remembering event sequences. In P. van den Broek, P. J. Bauer, & T. Bourg (Eds.), *Event comprehension and representation* (pp. 237–270). Hillsdale, NJ: Lawrence Erlbaum Associates, Inc.

Trabasso, T., van den Broek, P., & Suh, S. (1989). Logical necessity and transitivity of causal relations in stories. *Discourse Processes, 12,* 1–25.

APPENDIX

Script, Counterscript Ironic, Anomaly–Unexpected Event Stories for Planned-Loss Ironic Kind in Birthday Theme

Setting

1. At his birthday party, Billy gets a telescope to see the moon.

Goal

2. Billy wants to be real sure that nothing bad happens to his great new telescope present.

3. He wants to be sure that the kids don't fool around with it and break it or that nothing spills on it during his birthday party.

Idea

4. So he decides he'd better put it in his bedroom closet right away because it won't get bothered in there.

Crisis

5. But all the kids want Billy to stay in his living room and open the rest of his presents.

Resolution

6. So Billy tells his friends that they can go ahead and open a present for him and he'll be right back.

Goal-Directed Actions

7. The kids say "okay" and start opening one of Billy's presents.
8. Billy picks up his telescope very carefully and starts walking to his room.

Outcome

Script

9. He gets to his room, opens his closet door, and places the telescope safely in his closet.
10. Billy's friends yell to him to hurry up and so he runs back to them.
11. He opens all the rest of his birthday presents.

Counterscript Ironic

9. Just as he gets near his room, he trips and drops the telescope smack on the floor.
10. Billy picks up the telescope and looks through it, but can't see anything at all.
11. The telescope is all broken and no good anymore.

Anomaly–Unexpected

9. As he gets near his room, he hears the kids screaming so he runs back to them.
10. He sees his friends are having a really big fight, yelling and hitting each other.
11. They're really mad and ruining his happy birthday party.

Emotion Reaction

Script

12. Billy is very happy.

Counterscript Ironic and Anomaly–Unexpected

12. Billy is very sad.

JOURNAL OF COGNITION AND DEVELOPMENT, 3(1), 117–118

Books Received from August 1, 2000 to August 1, 2001

Brain, Vision, Memory: Tales in the History of Neuroscience (1998). C. G. Gross. Cambridge, MA: MIT Press. 255 pp. Paperback, no price given.

Of Children: An Introduction to Child and Adolescent Development (9th ed., 2001). G. R. Lefrancois. Belmont, CA: Wadsworth/Thomson Learning. 654 pp. Hardcover, no price given.

Cognitive Rehabilitation in Old Age (2000). R. D. Hill, L. Backman, & A. Stigsdotter Neely (Eds.). New York: Oxford University Press. 299 pp. Cloth, $55.00.

Complex Cognition: The Psychology of Human Thought (2001). R. J. Sternberg & T. Ben-Zeev. Oxford: Oxford University Press. 450 pp. Hardcover, no price given.

Consciousness & Emotion (2000). R. D. Ellis & N. Newton (Eds.). Volume 1, Issue 1. Philadelphia: John Benjamins. 191 pp. Paperback, no price given.

The Development of Implicit and Explicit Memory (2000). C. Rovee-Collier, H. Hayne, & M. Colombo. A Volume in a Series: Advances in Consciousness Research. Philadelphia: John Benjamins. 322 pp. Paperback, $39.95.

Developmental Disorders of the Frontostriatal System: Neuropsychological, Neuropsychiatric, and Evolutionary Perspectives (2001). J. L. Bradshaw. A Volume in a Series: Brain Damage, Behaviour and Cognition. Philadelphia: Psychology Press. 320 pp. Cloth, $59.95.

Exploring Science: The Cognition & Development of Discovery Processes (1999). D. Klahr. Cambridge, MA: MIT Press. 276 pp. Cloth, $56.25.

The Future of Career (2000). A. Collin & R. A. Young. New York: Cambridge University Press. 321 pp. Paperback, $22.95.

Handbook of Clinical Child Psychology (3rd ed., 2001). C. E. Walker & M. C. Roberts. New York: Wiley. 1177 pp. Hardcover, no price given.

Handbook of Developmental Cognitive Neuroscience (2001). C. A. Nelson & M. Luciana. Cambridge, MA: MIT Press. 685 pp. Hardcover, no price given.

Hemispheric Asymmetry: What's Right and What's Left (2001). J. B. Hellige. A Volume in a Series: Perspectives in Cognitive Neuroscience. Cambridge, MA: Harvard University Press. 396 pp. Paperback, no price given.

How Children Learn the Meaning of Words (2000). P. Bloom. Cambridge, MA: MIT Press. 569 pp. Cloth, $59.25.

Identity's Architect: A Biography of Erik H. Erikson (2000). L. J. Freedman. Cambridge, MA: Harvard University Press. 592 pp. Paperback, $19.95.

Infancy: Infant, Family, and Society (4th ed., 2001). A. Fogel. Belmont, CA: Wadsworth/Thomson Learning. 556 pp. Paperback, no price given.

The Infant's World (2001). P. Rochat. A Volume in a Series: The Developing Child. Cambridge, MA: Harvard University Press. 262 pp. Hardcover, $29.95.

Intentions and Intentionality: Foundations of Social Cognition (2001). B. F. Malle, L. J. Moses, & D. A. Baldwin. Cambridge, MA: MIT Press. 417 pp. Hardcover, no price given.

Lucy's Legacy: Sex and Intelligence in Human Evolution (2001). A. Jolly. Cambridge, MA: Harvard University Press. 518 pp. Paperback, $18.95.

Minds, Brains, and Learning: Understanding the Psychological and Educational Relevance of Neuro-scientific Research (2001). J. P. Bynes. New York: Guilford. 214 pp. Paperback, $25.00.

Motivation: A Biobehavioural Approach (2000). R. Wong. New York: Cambridge University Press. 281 pp. Paperback, $29.95.

Pathways to Language: From Fetus to Adolescent (2001). K. Karmiloff & A. Karmiloff-Smith. A Volume in a Series: The Developing Child. Cambridge, MA: Harvard University Press. 256 pp. Hardcover, $27.95.

Quantitative Data Analysis with SPSS Release 10 for Windows (2001). A. Bryman & D. Cramer. Philadelphia: Psychology Press. 336 pp. Paperback, $29.95.

The Science of Learning (2001). J. J. Pear. Philadelphia: Psychology Press. 536 pp. Paperback, $39.95.

Simple Heuristics That Make Us Smart (1999). G. Gigerenzer, P. M. Todd, & the ABC Research Group. Oxford: Oxford University Press. 416 pp. Paperback, price not given.

The Social Context of Cognitive Development (2000). M. Gauvain. New York: Guilford. 249 pp. Paperback, $22.00.

The Social Mind: Construction of the Idea (2000). J. Valsiner & R. Van der Veer. New York: Cambridge University Press. 488 pp. Hardback, $69.95.

Technology in Action (2000). C. Heath & P. Luff. New York: Cambridge University Press. 269 pp. Hardback, $69.95.

Three Seductive Ideas (2000). J. Kagan. Cambridge, MA: Harvard University Press. 240 pp. Paperback, $22.95.

Workplace Studies: Recovering Work Practice and Informing System Design (2000). P. Luff, J. Hindmarsh, & C. Heath. New York: Cambridge University Press. 283 pp. Paperback, $24.95.

Unity and Modularity in the Mind and the Self: Studies on the Relationships Between Self-Awareness, Personality, and Intellectual Development from Childhood to Adolescence (2000). A. Demetriou & S. Kazi. Anover: Taylor & Francis. 252 pp. Hardback, $60.00.

Vulnerability to Psychopathology: Risks Across the Lifespan (2000). R. E. Ingram & J. M. Price. New York: Guilford. 476 pp. Hardcover, $55.00.

For Product Safety Concerns and Information please contact our EU representative GPSR@taylorandfrancis.com Taylor & Francis Verlag GmbH, Kaufingerstraße 24, 80331 München, Germany

Batch number: 08153776

Printed by Printforce, the Netherlands